For Seán

Colm Keane's 22 books include the number one bestsellers *Going Home: Irish Stories from the Edge of Death*, *Padre Pio: The Irish Connection* and *Nervous Breakdown*. He is a graduate of Trinity College, Dublin, and Georgetown University, Washington DC. As a broadcaster, he won a Jacob's Award and a Glaxo Fellowship for European Science Writers. His books, spanning nine chart bestsellers, include the recently-published *The Distant Shore* and *Forewarned*.

CONTENTS

I looked over Jordan, and what did I see,
Coming for to carry me home?
A band of angels coming after me,
Coming for to carry me home.

> 'Swing Low, Sweet Chariot', African-American
> spiritual, its composition often credited to freed
> slave Wallis Willis sometime before 1862.

INTRODUCTION

Few thoughts are more distressing than those regarding how we will die. Will our dying be painful, traumatic and frightening, sad or lonely? Will we die with dignity and at peace or struggle with discomfort and despair? Will we be alone or with loved ones? Perhaps, more importantly, will we be confronted by a dark, deathly void or face a joyous journey to another world, another sphere of existence, where we will meet once again those who have already departed?

There is, at least, one dramatic and comforting phenomenon that will almost certainly be experienced by all of us shortly before we die. Most often, it involves visits from relatives and friends who have passed on before us. Less frequently, it involves visitations from religious figures or glimpses of beautiful landscapes. These powerful and intriguing – perhaps even breathtaking and thrilling – pre-death happenings are commonly referred to as 'deathbed visions'.

Dating back to the earliest recorded time and no doubt to the beginning of mankind, deathbed visions are the most frequently reported – and most widely witnessed – of all death phenomena. Ask anyone who has observed one and they will describe a profound sense of amazement at what they have seen. Witness one, as you sit by a dying person, and you will be overwhelmed by the sense of peace, calmness and tranquillity that characterises the final hours or minutes of those who are passing away.

Deathbed visions, however, are not exclusively about happy

1

reconciliations, but have a 'takeaway purpose'. 'My mother has come for me,' 'She's bringing me with her,' 'I'm joining her now' are commonly reported remarks. The intention is clear – to guide and welcome the dying and to escort them away. Although those who appear bring comfort and peace, more importantly they offer assistance in the transition from this world to the next.

These visions are of enormous significance and provide us with credible evidence that we may live on after death. How can the dead reappear unless they have survived physical extinction? How do they so predictably arrive at their loved ones' final moments? Does not their offer of welcome and guidance imply that an afterlife exists? Above all, how come the visits, as commonly observed and described, seem so genuine, convincing and real?

In the course of writing my two recent books on near-death experiences, *Going Home* and *The Distant Shore*, I encountered a remarkable similarity between the meetings described during deathbed visions and one of the elements reported during near-death experiences. Although the near-death phenomenon – where people die temporarily and are revived – involves experiences of tunnels, bright lights, encounters with a superior being and life reviews, those who return from them also report meetings with deceased family and friends.

Former loved ones arrive to greet them, resulting in joyous reunions. Separated by a border, such as a bridge, river, lake or sometimes a veil, the deceased normally stand on the far side of the boundary awaiting those about to cross over. The people approaching from this world are delighted to see them. The dead, in turn, are welcoming. They often tell those who arrive that it is 'not their time,' resulting in a return to real life.

It is clear that both of these experiences – the encounters with the deceased during the near-death experience and the deathbed vision – are essentially one and the same thing. Both involve meetings with lost loved ones. Both occur at the time of death. Both almost always bring solace and comfort to the individual who is passing away. For these reasons, encounters with deceased relatives and friends during near-death experiences are also addressed in the pages ahead.

Ultimately, this book does not provide proof of 'heaven', nor does it attempt to do so. However, it does provide a convincing case that something of us survives after we die, be it our soul, spirit, mind or consciousness, whatever that entity might be. Somehow, it seems, the moment when our brain flatlines, our heart stops beating and we are declared clinically dead is not the end of the story.

It is for another book to speculate on what shape or form our future existence, if any, might take – perhaps reincarnation or maybe continuation in a different dimension such as a paradise, heaven, Elysium, Valhalla, Tír na nÓg, Hy-Brasil or parallel universe, where we live on in the company of those we once shared our lives with on earth.

In the meantime, we can learn about what faces us in our transition to whatever that world might be by examining the most amazing phenomena relating to death – those startling, dazzling moments when the dying meet again those they once knew and loved as part of their final passage to the other side.

Colm Keane

JOYOUS REUNIONS

One Saturday morning, in early 1998, a woman named Jan was seated at her dying mother's bedside in County Donegal. The mother was propped up on pillows, wearing a pale-blue knitted bed jacket and was sipping a cup of warm tea. Although dying from old age, she was sharp and alert. She was still reading books, her latest being a prayer book. On this Saturday morning, however, she was staring vacantly into space.

Suddenly, a most beautiful smile came over her face. Her countenance lit up and her eyes opened wide. She said to her daughter, 'There's your dad!' She stretched out one arm, with her hand open wide, as if reaching for someone. Her daughter thought she was stretching for the teacup, but she wasn't. She looked, but she couldn't see anyone.

The mother spoke once more to her daughter. 'Did you see him?' she asked. 'Yes,' her daughter replied, unwilling to admit she saw nothing. Her mother then said, 'Isn't he looking good?' The daughter replied, 'Yes, he is.' All this time, the mother's eyes were wide open as she gazed at this astonishing sight.

That was the full extent of their conversation. 'It was the smile on her face that really caught my attention,' the daughter revealed afterwards. 'It was as if her face was glowing. And I clearly remember that her big, wide-open eyes were as blue as could be.'

The woman soon fell asleep and didn't wake up the

following day. She died on the Monday evening at six o'clock. 'I believe that she saw my father,' the daughter remarked. 'I have absolutely no doubt in my mind. Even after all these years, it has stayed vividly with me. I never thought deeply about it, but I do believe there is something beyond life. I think there has to be, especially after experiencing something like that.'

What the woman from County Donegal experienced back in 1998 was unquestionably a deathbed vision. Like many individuals who are fading away, she saw deceased family welcoming her to the other side. Usually, these are familiar people who were once closely known and loved, such as dead parents, spouses, children or friends. Less commonly, people report seeing angels or religious figures. The dying may also witness scenes of great tranquillity and peace, involving beautiful landscapes, intense light and many vivid colours.

These visions have a profound impact on those who are passing away. They normally bring serenity, contentment, peace of mind and result in a 'good death'. Apprehensions and fear disappear. Pain eases and is replaced by a soothing calmness. Those who are suffering suddenly pick up. The dispirited reveal a sense of supreme elation. They are heartened, reassured and happy.

The dying also look pleased at the prospect of going with those who have come to greet them. They relish the journey they now know is ahead. Their demeanour is full of hope and expectation. Many are so overjoyed that they don't want to come back. Occasionally, they ask doctors to stop trying to save them. There is a huge sense of consolation knowing they will soon be with dear-departed relatives and friends in a better world.

'Suddenly, my grandmother opened her eyes,' Lynn, who lives near the Cork/Limerick border, said of her grand-mother's deathbed vision involving two deceased brothers. 'She had these vibrant, blue, piercing eyes. She literally sat up and she smiled. She looked straight ahead of her and she said, 'Oh! Jim! Tom! There you are! I can go now!' Those were her two closest brothers, who were dead long before.

'She was looking straight down to the bottom of the bed, where none of us was standing. It was the most beautiful thing I have ever witnessed in my life. It was just amazing. She then just closed her eyes and went to sleep and passed on to Jim and Tom. I felt all was well and my grandmother was safe home.'

A notable feature of deathbed visions is the 'gaze' or 'stare' often seen on the faces of those who are fading away. Their eyes focus unwaveringly on some distant sight. They concentrate intently, amazed or bewildered by the people or images they are seeing. Sometimes, they call out the names of those coming to greet them. Other times, they reach out or smile. They always seem satisfied, pleased or even ecstatic as they stare fixedly ahead.

Perhaps the most powerful description of this propensity to 'gaze' came from the pen of the respected nineteenth-century Anglo-Irish author Frances Power Cobbe. Born into land-owning stock and in later life a friend of Charles Darwin, she wrote a book in 1882 called *The Peak in Darien*, which espoused her views on personal immortality. It contained a graphic outline of a dying person's demeanour while exper-iencing a vision.

'The dying person is lying quietly,' Cobbe wrote, 'when suddenly, in the very act of expiring, he looks up – sometimes starts up in bed – and gazes on (what appears to be) vacancy, with an expression of astonishment, sometimes developing instantly into joy, and sometimes cut short in the first emotion of solemn wonder and awe.

'If the dying man were to see some utterly-unexpected but instantly-recognised vision, causing him a great surprise, or rapturous joy, his face could not better reveal the fact. The very instant this phenomenon occurs, death is actually taking place, and the eyes glaze even while they gaze at the un-known sight.'

Examples of this steely, intense focus Cobbe so accurately and succinctly describes are common. 'My mother sat straight up in the bed. Her two eyes opened wide,' Marie, from County Waterford, said regarding the expression on her 90-year-old mother's face as she passed away. 'She was looking straight ahead of her, slightly up a bit, but not focused on anybody. She was gazing ahead at this wonder. And she had a big smile. We were all astounded. We all knew straightaway that somebody had come to meet her. After about 20 seconds, she just fell back and she was gone.'

Not surprisingly, profound effects may be felt by those who witness the dying in this way. Many say the occurrence brings them a great sense of peace. Knowing that pain has been replaced by elation provides wonderful solace. They are pleased that their relatives are happy as they fade away. Afterlife beliefs are often intensified following the experience.

'I would never be afraid to die after it,' Marie, from County Waterford, remarked. 'Before, at the thought of dying, I'd panic. But now, I wouldn't. I know that I'll be going some-where. I always had a belief about life after death, but that proved it for me. I know there's more to it than just dying. I also know that people come back. And I know I will meet my mother and other relatives again someday.'

It would be facile to speculate on the precise numbers of those confronting death who experience a deathbed vision. Focusing solely on those who are conscious before dying, one estimate suggests that a figure of around 50 – 60 per cent might be close to the mark. Although other estimates differ, a study of the statistics indicates that somewhere in the region of one-half to two-thirds of those who are alert prior to their deaths might experience them.

That this figure is most likely correct is evident from the observations of relatives and health-care professionals. An Irish hospice study, which included responses from doctors and nurses, social workers, chaplains and care assistants, revealed some 62 per cent saying that deathbed phenomena had been related to them by relatives, with 65 per cent saying that deathbed phenomena had been related to them by a patient. Clearly, visions are common.

Deathbed visions, however, are likely to be far more prevalent than these figures suggest. To begin with, not all people are conscious shortly before they pass away. Many are either comatose or sedated, while others die following car crashes, heart attacks or other abrupt events. It follows, therefore, that the number of dying people who are capable of sharing their visions openly with others will inevitably be limited.

It can also be conjectured that many of those who are dying will experience their visions while alone and not in the presence of family, friends or medical personnel. Their reactions or comments may therefore remain unnoticed. More may carry what they saw to their graves, with the experiences being so private or intense that they decide not to share them.

Observers nearby, such as family members or friends, may likewise dismiss or misinterpret what they are witnessing, regarding what they see as hallucinations or side-effects of medication and therefore never report them. How many people experience deathbed visions then? The answer can never be known. It might, instead, be fair to speculate that, if they are what they appear to be, we will all experience one of our own – it's just that formal evidence to support this assertion does not exist.

We know more clearly from studies and anecdotally how long the experiences persist and how soon afterwards the person dies. About one-half of all experiences last for five minutes or less, with two-thirds lasting less than 15 minutes, according to a landmark study published in 1977 by the eminent psychology researchers Dr. Karlis Osis and Dr. Erlendur Haraldsson. Their study concluded that the visions are a reasonable indicator of imminent death, with over one-quarter dying within an hour and the majority dying within a day. They are also experienced by people of all ages, sexes and creeds.

An additional feature of visions is the 'crowded room' syndrome, whereby those who are dying may report the arrival of numerous people who have already departed. Cases involving the arrival of a multitude of deceased family members or other dead people – not all of them instantly recognisable to the ailing person – are regularly reported. One distinguished researcher, David Kessler, heard so many references to the words 'crowd' or 'crowded' in the stories he encountered that he suggested our deaths might well be a 'standing-room only' experience.

It is also occasionally reported that people in attendance at another person's death may somehow participate in that person's deathbed vision. Although relatively rare, cases have been documented where a family member or friend who is present in the room can also clearly see the visionary figures.

Alternatively, a strange light or mist may be seen or energy sensed. Unusual cases where an energy cloud forms over the dying person and then drifts away at the time of death have also been noted.

One classic example of a 'shared' deathbed vision involved a 17-year-old girl, Laura, who was dying. A hospital staff member, who knew the girl well, observed the following: 'A short time before she expired I became aware that two spirit forms were standing by the bedside, one on either side of it. I did not see them enter the room; they were standing by the bedside when they first became visible to me, but I could see them as distinctly as I could any of the human occupants of the room.

'I recognised their faces as those of two girls who had been the closest friends of the girl who was dying. They had passed away a year before and were then about her own age. Just before they appeared the dying girl exclaimed, "It has grown suddenly dark; I cannot see anything!" But she recognised them immediately. A smile, beautiful to see, lit up her face.' Laura then stretched out her hands and said, 'Oh, you have come to take me away!' Shortly afterwards, she died.

Contrary to the objections of sceptics, available evidence suggests that those who experience deathbed visions are rational, lucid and aware of their surroundings at the time the visions take place. Their observations are coherent and differ from the ramblings associated with sickness. They are clearly not hallucinatory. Unlike hallucinations, which usually feature either living persons or bizarre characters, the visions primarily concern known, deceased family members. These factors will be examined in detail in the final chapter.

Again, in contrast to the protestations of sceptics, the majority of those who see visions are not on medication.

Studies also show that those who are prescribed drugs such as morphine or other pain relievers do not have a more pronounced tendency to experience visions than those not on these drugs. Nor is religious conviction or affiliation seen as contributory; in fact, the content of visions is often contrary to conventional religious beliefs. Once again, these issues will be scrutinised in the final chapter.

Children also experience deathbed visions. Early examples involving young people were recorded as far back as the late nineteenth century and early twentieth century by Sir William Fletcher Barrett, a Jamaica-born scientist who was appointed Professor of Physics at the esteemed Royal College of Science in Dublin. Throughout his most distinguished career, Barrett attempted to fuse the scientific principles of physics with the spiritual laws of God. 'Science reveals the garment of God, religion the heart of God' was how he articulated his personal philosophy.

Among the many case histories recounted by Barrett in his groundbreaking book *Death-Bed Visions*, which was first published in 1926, was a story involving a young girl dying from diphtheria. In the course of telling her mother how to dispose of her few personal belongings, the girl suddenly became alert. Gazing at the ceiling at the far side of the room, and after looking steadily and listening intently for a short time, she said, 'Yes, Grandma, I am coming, only wait just a little while, please.'

Her father asked her, 'Do you see your grandma?' He was aware that her grandmother had died a few years earlier and that the two had been close friends. Surprised at the question, she responded, 'Can't you see her? She is right there waiting for me.' The girl once more turned her attention to the disposal of her few belongings. Having finished, she fixed her eyes on the vision and said, 'Yes, Grandma, I'm coming now.' She then died.

Back in 1906, Barrett chronicled another childhood case history, this time detailing the death of a young boy aged nine. The boy, we are informed, had recently undergone an operation from which he had failed to recover. Despite his condition, he was perfectly rational and lucid, fully aware of the presence of his mother, the nurse and the doctor.

Knowing he was dying, the boy held his mother's hands. After a short time, he looked up and asked her if she too could see his 'little sister' in the room. 'No, where is she?' his mother asked, aware that his sister had died four years before his birth. 'Right over there. She is looking at me,' he responded.

The boy then exclaimed that he could see a deceased adult acquaintance along with a young friend who had died about a year beforehand. 'I'm going to them,' he said. 'I don't want to leave you, but you'll come to me soon, won't you? Open the door and let them in. They are waiting outside.' Immediately after saying this, he died.

Barrett recorded further childhood narratives, which he believed offered the strongest support for the authenticity of deathbed visions. He was particularly interested in how some children described angels. 'We always thought the angels had wings!' one young child, named Daisy, who was dying, said to her sister. 'But it is a mistake; they don't have any.'

When questioned by her sister how angels could fly down from heaven without wings, Daisy responded, 'Oh, but they don't fly, they just come.' Such remarks, which were not uncommon, were so dramatically out of kilter with the religious imagery of the time, where all angels had wings, that Barrett suggested they could not be flights of fancy.

The most convincing support for the veracity of deathbed visions undoubtedly arises when those who are passing away describe visitations from people they could not have known had died. Sometimes, the information about the recent death of a friend or relative has been kept from the dying person so as not to unduly upset them. Other times – especially long ago, prior to telephones and other modern communication methods – news might not yet have arrived from far away confirming the other person's demise. As a consequence, the dying person is normally surprised by the visitation.

Instances are widely reported. For example, the author Frances Power Cobbe recalled a case in the late nineteenth century in which a dying woman identified three of her long-deceased brothers as having appeared to her on her deathbed. Surprisingly, however, the woman also identified a fourth brother, who had been living in India and was presumed to be still very much alive.

Cobbe remarked: 'The coupling of his name with that of his dead brothers excited such awe and horror in the mind of one of the persons present that she rushed from the room. In due course of time letters were received announcing the death of the brother in India, which had occurred some time before his dying sister seemed to recognise him.'

A further case was recorded in the late 1870s, involving a Miss Harriet Ogle. Her story, which was chronicled by the Society for Psychical Research in the UK, outlined how her brother John, while dying in 1879, reported not only seeing a different brother Joe, who was already deceased, but also an acquaintance who he could not have known had died.

'About an hour before he expired,' Miss Ogle wrote, 'he saw his brother – who had died about 16 years before – and John, looking up with fixed interest, said, "Joe! Joe!" and immediately after exclaimed with ardent surprise, "George Hanley!"' Miss Ogle's mother, who was also present, having arrived from a location some 40 miles away where George Hanley lived, was astonished. Not only had Mr. Hanley died ten days before, but the mother was the only person present who was aware of his death.

Yet another classic example was recorded by Sir William Barrett in *Death-Bed Visions*, involving a woman who was dying from heart failure following the delivery of her child. The case, which was included in my previous books *Going Home* and *The Distant Shore,* was witnessed by Barrett's wife – the obstetric surgeon Lady Barrett – and also by the resident medical officer and the matron of the hospital the woman was attending, together with the dying woman's mother.

Focusing her attention intently on one particular spot in the room, the woman exclaimed, 'Why, it's Father! Oh, he's so glad I'm coming; he is so glad.' She continued, 'I can see Father; he wants me, he is so lonely. I am coming.' She added, 'Oh, he is so near.' Then, with a rather puzzled expression, she exclaimed to her mother, 'He has Vida with him.' Staring directly at her mother, she once more said in astonishment, 'Vida is with him.'

Vida was the dying woman's sister, who had passed away more than two weeks earlier. The woman, however, had not been informed of this tragic development. Instead, the family had acceded to a request from the matron and carefully withheld the information due to the seriousness of the patient's condition. Even letters were censored, as her mother later confirmed in written testimony.

For the record, the unfortunate young woman – referred to in Barrett's book *Death-Bed Visions* as 'Mrs. B.', although we know her first name was Doris – died on 12 January 1924, two weeks and four days after the death of her sister Vida, who departed the world on Christmas Day 1923.

As mentioned in the introduction to this book, what is also interesting about deathbed visions is the manner in which they so closely resemble one of the prominent features of the near-death experience. Of the many happenings associated with a near-death journey – a phenomenon which may result, for example, from a heart attack, car crash or near drowning – one of the most intriguing is the meeting with deceased family or friends.

Having departed from their bodies, those who temporarily 'die' normally feel calm and at peace, travel through a dark tunnel with a bright light at the end, reach a border or a boundary, encounter a 'superior being', undergo a life review and face a decision to either stay or come back. They also meet their dear departed. These joyous reconciliations, which are remarkably similar to deathbed visions, have been reported in a multitude of cultures since time immemorial.

One story, which was featured in *Going Home*, illustrates the distinct parallels. The story involves a woman named Sarah, from County Donegal, who had a vivid near-death experience while undergoing an operation in hospital. Reflecting all the exuberance of a deathbed vision, she was overjoyed with the people she saw and couldn't wait to join them even though she was unable to identify them.

'Three people were coming towards me,' she recalled. 'They were very old and in human form. I knew for a fact that their purpose was to come for me. I wanted to go to them, as if they were long-lost relatives or ancestors or friends or something. It was an overwhelming desire. I definitely felt a great empathy with them. I felt they were my kindred. I was so anxious to go to them and I didn't want to come back.'

Another woman, Paula, from County Waterford, who had a near-death experience during an illness, was overjoyed to see her deceased grandfather. 'He was standing in front of the light,' she remembered in *The Distant Shore*. 'His role was to help me over, to be there as a guide. I was very happy to see him. He was a really nice man. I had loved him madly. Around him were lots of other people or "spirits" or what I would call "others" who were going to help me as well.'

In most of these cases, the deceased relatives or friends are seen on the far side of a dividing line separating life from death. This border or boundary is often a bridge, river or lake. Sometimes, it is a curtain or veil. Other times, it is the light at the tunnel's end. In the stories related to me, those who are arriving generally don't cross over the partition. Should they do so, they would move to the other side, thus ruling out a return to life.

'Blowing in front of me was what I can only describe as a linen panel or a curtain,' said one woman, Michelle, from County Galway, who had a near-death experience during a difficult childbirth. 'As I got to the end of the panel or curtain, I floated past it to the side, but didn't cross the line. Just beyond the line were my mother-in-law and father-in-law, who had both passed away. They were standing not too far away, but far enough that I couldn't touch them. They just stood there smiling and looking at me.'

Another person, Jimmy, from County Wexford, saw his sister and his father-in-law, who were both dead, on the far side of a river, with their hands joined. Once again, he never crossed the divide. 'They beckoned me to come across,' he explained. 'I had the feeling I was going into a new life. I went into the water and started to swim.'

The hands of his sister and father-in-law suddenly parted, revealing a God-like figure behind them. 'I put up my hands to touch the form with outstretched hands. But when just a finger-length from touching the hands, I started to go back-wards. I came back to life again,' he said.

As pointed out in the introduction, it is noticeable that the encounters with deceased people described in both near-death experiences and deathbed visions are one and the same thing. In both cases, people are actually passing away at the time these events occur. Likewise, in both cases, deceased relatives or friends arrive to meet the dying, to greet them and welcome them to the other side.

There are, however, a few very important differences. In sharp contrast to deathbed visions, the relatives who appear during near-death experiences often tell those who are arriving, 'Go back, it is not your time.' What happened to Charles, from County Roscommon, is a case in point. He encountered a large number of people who not only seemed to be judging him, but who advised him he had to return.

'They all started looking at each other and shaking their heads,' he said. 'It was like they were saying, "He's not going to be allowed to stay." I felt a great sense of loss or dis-appointment. I had the feeling I was going to have to go back and that's exactly what I did.'

Michelle, from County Galway, who we heard from earlier, was similarly advised that it wasn't her time despite her perilous state during a most difficult childbirth. 'When I saw them (her mother-in-law and father-in-law), I went to go over,' she remarked. 'But my mother-in-law, Barbara, put both her hands up as if to say, "Stop!" She shook her head very kindly, as if to say, "Not now! Go back!" I thought of my baby and knew I had to return.'

Another big difference is that in the case of near-death experiences, those who die temporarily – and, so, don't cross over – remain separated from the departed by the border or boundary mentioned earlier. In the deathbed vision, by way of contrast, the dying almost never speak of a border or boundary, perhaps because they are on their final journeys and won't be returning. The border is of negligible interest. Instead, they focus on the approaching dead relatives or religious figureheads who come to help them on their way.

Furthermore, in the case of a near-death experience, either through natural good fortune or medical intervention, the person eventually returns to real life. This is not so in the case of a deathbed vision. Despite these few differences, both phenomena unquestionably share fundamental elements in common. It is for this reason that a chapter of new stories involving the appearance of relatives during near-death experiences is included later in this book.

Returning exclusively to the issue of deathbed visions, although the publication of Sir William Barrett's ground-breaking *Death-Bed Visions* back in 1926 excited enormous interest in the topic, the truth is that knowledge of the phenomenon has been around certainly since the beginning of recorded time and probably since the very beginning of mankind itself. The earliest landmark studies on the topic – D. P. Kidder's *The Dying Hours of Good and Bad Men Contrasted*, published in 1848, and James H. Hyslop's *Psychical Research and the Resurrection*, published in 1908 – made many waves, although they never matched Barrett's impact.

From the sixteenth to the nineteenth centuries, deathbed visions also featured extensively in many plays and novels. William Shakespeare was among those who alluded to the phenomenon. For example, his celebrated comic character Falstaff in *Henry V* – a play believed to have been written around 1599 – was reported to have 'babbled of green fields' at the time of his death.

Victorian literary figures, writing from the late 1830s up to the beginning of the twentieth century, had an even more intense preoccupation with the topic. In his book *The Life and Adventures of Nicholas Nickleby*, which was published in 1839, Charles Dickens attributed a deathbed vision to one of his characters, the frail and simple Smike. Struck down with tuberculosis, Smike was held in his friend Nicholas's arms as he faded away.

'He fell into a slight slumber,' we are told, 'and waking, smiled as before; then spoke of beautiful gardens, which he said stretched out before him, and were filled with figures of men, women, and many children, all with light upon their faces; then whispered that it was Eden – and so died.'

Eleven years later, in 1850, the elderly British poet laureate William Wordsworth experienced a real-life deathbed vision. Aged 80, he had already lost several of his children to illness, but none more regretfully than his beloved daughter Dora, who died of tuberculosis. Following her death, he planted hundreds of daffodils in her memory in a field, which to this day is called 'Dora's Field'. On his deathbed, in April 1850, he was heard to call out, 'God bless you! Is that you, Dora?'

Three years further on, in 1853, another graphic deathbed vision was described by Elizabeth Gaskell in her novel *Ruth*. Gaskell showed a keen appreciation of the phenomenon when describing Ruth's death as follows: 'Suddenly she opened wide her eyes, and gazed intently forwards, as if she saw some happy vision, which called out a lovely, rapturous, breathless smile. "The Light is coming," she said. And, raising herself slowly, she stretched out her arms, and then fell back, very still for evermore.'

Almost midway into the following century, in 1944, future country music legend Johnny Cash lost his older brother Jack in a tragic work-related accident. The unfortunate event involved a saw which almost cut him in two in the mill where he was employed. It took him over a week to die. Johnny, who was then only 12 years old, later claimed in his autobiography that he along with his brother and mother had a feeling of foreboding on the day of the disastrous mishap. He also described how the 15-year-old Jack said on his deathbed that he had visions of heaven and angels.

Moving on to the twenty-first century, Apple computer company founder Steve Jobs had a vision while he was dying from pancreatic cancer. The computer innovator had suffered from a rare form of the disease, only to finally succumb in October 2011 after an eight-year battle. Although it is not known exactly what he witnessed on his deathbed, his sister Mona, who was present, described how he looked for a long time at his wife and children and then over their shoulders past them. His final words, as he gazed into the distance, were, 'Oh, wow! Oh, wow! Oh, wow!'

Despite numerous investigations and books, not to mention many thousands of years of observing them, deathbed visions remain a topic of heated debate. Sceptics, on the one hand, argue that they result from any number of factors including oxygen deprivation, sleep deprivation, medication, delirium, religious fervour and wish-fulfilment. All you have to do is believe in deathbed reconciliations, some sceptics say, and the dying brain will grant your wishes. These arguments will be examined later in the book.

Proponents of deathbed visions, on the other hand, say that they are not only real, but they clearly establish that death is a transitory process, a rite of passage whereby we seamlessly move from one world to the next and, in the process of doing so, are reconciled with those we once knew and loved. Should they be right, then deathbed visions may be one of the most cogent arguments for survival after death, establishing the case for the existence of a better life, a better world beyond the horizon. It is to stories of this persuasion that we first turn our attention.

DEATHBED VISIONS

The stories you are about to read, although modern, are as old as mankind. They have featured in almost all cultures and religions stretching back through the ages. They reach back in time to Jesus Christ who, according to third-century legends, paid a deathbed visit to his mother, the Virgin Mary, shortly before she died. They extend right through the eighth century, when the author and scholar Bede described how a recently-deceased holy man visited a dying nun and told her that she would expire the following morning, which she did.

The idea that visiting relatives or other figures help 'guide' those who are dying is also old. The ancient Jewish Kabbalah describes how at a man's death 'his father and his relatives gather round him, and he sees them and recognizes them … and they accompany his soul to the place where it is to abide.' Similar guides feature in Buddhism, where those unprepared to enter the light meet with angels who direct them. Early priests who claimed to communicate with the gods, known as shamans, were said to have travelled between the real world and the spirit world and to have guided the dying on their journeys following death.

The concept that we will all be reunited in an afterlife likewise has ancient roots. Jesus alluded to it on the cross, promising one of the thieves who was dying beside him, 'Truly, I say to you, today you will be with me in paradise.' In Islam, a person joins others in heaven, such as parents, wives and children, if their good deeds on earth outweigh their sins. In Hinduism, heaven is occupied by liberated souls who live on in beautiful, youthful forms.

Cree Indians also report incidents very similar to what you are about to read, with a witness to a 20-year-old's death describing how he 'suddenly sat up, stretched forth his arms in a yearning gesture, while an ecstatic smile broke over his face. It was not simply a smile of pleasure, but something far beyond it. The veil was lifted, and no one who was looking on could fail to realize that it was a glorious vision that met his gaze.'

All of the above-mentioned elements are present in the following pages; the only differences being their modern roots and that the stories are purely Irish. Their fundamental basis, however, is familiar: that our deceased loved ones arrive to help us at the time of our deaths and that some aspect of our being – our mind, spirit, soul, consciousness, call it whatever you wish – moves on to another plane of existence where we all meet again.

TONY, FROM CORK CITY, describes what his mother saw shortly before her death in 2002.

My mother got breast cancer in 2001. I will tell you the type of woman she was. On one occasion, when I went into the hospital to see her, she had a therapist coming in to explain to her about the cancer. The therapist wanted me to go away. My mum said to the therapist, 'Oh, no, it's alright. This is my son, Tony. I want you to explain to him that he's not to be put out over me losing my breast.' The therapist said, 'What do you mean?' My mother said, 'I'm afraid I can't breastfeed him anymore!' I was in my mid-50s at the time. She had a wicked sense of humour.

She survived the cancer. She flew through it. However,

about a year later, she decided to get her knees done. Her knees were always at her and she loved gardening. The operations went fine. She was due to come out from hospital on a Thursday, but she got a stroke. I wouldn't accept that she was not going to recover. Christmas passed and February arrived. It was then we were told that she was fading fast.

One weekend, things got very bad. On the Saturday, she slipped into a coma. She remained in the coma throughout Saturday and into the next day. On the Sunday, the doctors told us that she probably wouldn't last the night. We were there all that evening. I remember there were lots of noises going on in the hospital, with nurses running in and out to patients and things like that. I also remember that there was a television on in the next room, which was very loud. It must have been around seven or eight o'clock.

All of a sudden, the place became very quiet. Somebody turned down the television. There was a kind of grey light came into the room. It was like a pale light. I was sitting at the right-hand side of the bed. My youngest sister was sitting at the far side of the bed. My older sister was lying across the bed. The next thing, my mum looked up at me. She suddenly became more aware. She hadn't spoken clearly for a long time because of the stroke. She just said, 'Lift!'

I knew that she wanted to sit up. I lifted her up and I sat in behind her with my back up against the top of the bed. The next thing, she said, 'I can't go now! They are blocking me!' My grandfather was from the country and I knew from old stories that you should keep the curtains open when somebody is dying and nobody stands at the end of the bed. So I said to my sister, who was lying across the bed, 'Get off the bed.' She moved.

The next thing, my mother said, 'Look! There's Mum!' After that, she called out her father. She then called out each of her brothers, Seáno, Paddy, Christy, Willie, Jimmy. She also called out her sister Nancy. She then put her hand up to her face in surprise and she said, 'Oh! It's Brí!' I was puzzled by this, as I had never heard of a Brí before.

She continued, 'Jimmy, it's me, Mary!' I later discovered that Jimmy was only about eight years of age when he died. We said afterwards that my mother had got older since then, so she was introducing herself to him. She finished by saying, 'I'll see you all shortly!'

She was smiling as she said the names. She was happy and staring into the distance, down to the bottom of the bed. She was clearly delighted to see her family. It was as if she hadn't had a stroke. I couldn't really see her, as I was behind her. My sisters said to me afterwards, 'Her face was beautiful. It was the mum we could remember from when she was healthy.'

With that, she looked at me and indicated that she wanted to lie down again. The light came back into the room like normal. All the noise started again. It was as if we had been in some sort of different dimension altogether. I just turned around to my eldest sister and asked her, 'Who's Brí?' She said to me, 'Don't you know?' She then went on to explain, 'That was a sister you had who died about a month after she was born.' I think I would have been around six or seven at the time. That was the first I ever heard of this.

Later, when my father came over, I told him generally about what had happened. He said, 'Oh, come on!' It was only when we mentioned about Brí that he became startled. He said, 'Where did you hear that name from?' I told him what my mother had said. My father was country and, in the old days, when a child was born and died like that, they never spoke about it. My father suddenly got all upset and said, 'Oh, we don't talk about that!' I said, 'You have to tell me.' So he told me about Brí. It was amazing.

The following day, the priest came in, the bishop came in and they blessed my mother. It was a Monday. I remember the Angelus was striking. She was taking her last breaths at the time. I said, 'You watch, at the last stroke of the Angelus she will go.' When the last stroke came, her face became normal again, she had a lovely smile, she gave a deep sigh, she squeezed my hand and she was gone. She passed away on 18 February 2002.

My dad died on 12 June 2002, not long after my mother. Unfortunately, my dad died without us being there. I was sad about that because to be with the person and to see what we witnessed with my mother was a wonderful experience. I told a couple of my friends and they were stunned by it. They said, 'We wish we had that experience when our mums and dads were dying.'

I found what had happened with my mother was very reassuring and helpful and it made me understand what death is about. I believe what had occurred was that her family were coming to take her across. There is no doubt in my mind. She was contented and happy and was no longer traumatised by what she was going through. She wasn't hallucinating. She was rational and named out every single one of her family. I know she was happy to go with them to somewhere more peaceful.

It's also given me a great understanding regarding what life is about. Before that, I lived for each day only and would take each day as it comes. At work, at one time, I would get annoyed with people and bark and shout. Now, I don't. They look at me as if I have two heads and say, 'You're not giving out. Are you alright?'

It really has changed my attitude towards things. There's not a morning now that I don't sit on the edge of the bed and say, 'Thanks, God, for letting me get out of bed.' As my grandfather, who was a fluent Irish speaker, used to say from an old Irish saying, 'It's a great morning when you tie up your own bootlaces, but it's a better day when you take them off at night yourself.' I definitely appreciate life a lot better now after what I saw happen with my mum.

MARY, FROM COUNTY MAYO, witnessed her grandmother's deathbed vision back in 1970. Her grandmother was in her late 80s when she passed away.

My grandmother was the only one of my four grandparents I knew. The other three were dead when I was growing up. She was my mother's mother. She was a very hard-working woman and was widowed quite early. She was very kind and I would spend my holidays in her place. I would visit her maybe twice a year, up to when I was about 13 years of age.

We got on really well, so I loved going there. My mother was stricter and I didn't have the sort of fun with her that I had with my grandmother. The times with her were really happy, probably the happiest times of my life. Eventually, I went to secondary school and then started work in a hospital, where I didn't have much time off. As a result, I didn't see my grandmother quite so often.

About six months after I started work, I got this idea into my head that I should go to see my grandmother. She was in her late 80s at the time and had taken to the bed. She was old and failing, but not too bad at all. She had a son, who was a bachelor, living with her. She had a daughter, who lived in America, who had come home to visit. My mother was there at the time as well.

My brother drove me there in his black Morris Minor.

Having got there, I said, 'I'll stay the night and go back home tomorrow.' I had to get back as I was working the day after that again. So I stayed for the night. Everything was perfect. Everyone was there except for my brother, who decided to drive back home. I talked to my grandmother and looked after her. I gave her breakfast in the morning. I gave her mashed potatoes for her dinner. I then said, 'Gran, I have to go now. I have to get back for work.' So we said goodbye.

Her house was two miles outside of the nearby town. I had to walk to get to the town and then get what we used to call the 'mail car', or the post van, home. The bus had gone earlier in the morning, which was no use to me. There weren't many cars about in those days and don't forget my brother had already gone back home in his. So I set off walking up the road.

I was only gone about ten minutes when I saw my brother coming down the road in his black Morris Minor car. He pulled up and I said, 'I didn't know you were coming back.' He said, 'Well, I wasn't, but I just thought I would.' I was delighted and knew he would eventually give me a lift home. So I sat into the car and back we went to my grandmother's.

I came back into the house and saw my aunt and my mother in the kitchen. My uncle was down the fields, where he always was. I decided I would go straight down into my grandmother's room. I don't know why. I went over to the bed and said, 'Gran, I'm back for another while.' I don't know if she said anything in reply or not, but if she did it was very brief.

She then suddenly said, 'Look at the Blessed Virgin!' I said, 'Where?' She said, 'At the end of the bed!' while pointing right down to the bottom of the bed. I looked and couldn't see anything. She was lying very flat in the bed at the time and looked very frail. I didn't say anything because I couldn't see anything. I was surprised, but not afraid. I felt a sensation in the room.

The next thing, she rose up out of the bed with her hands stretched out. She said, as she rose up, 'Isn't she beautiful?' I think she thought I saw the Blessed Virgin. But I still said nothing. Overall, she said three times, 'Isn't she beautiful?' At this stage, she was elevated in the middle of the bed and sitting up. She looked like she was going to take-off from the bed and go through the roof. Without a doubt, something special was going on at that moment.

She had her eyes fixed, with a look of love on her face. She stared ahead and never looked at me. I was awfully surprised. It felt like this went on for a long time, like five minutes, but I know that it must have all lasted only about a minute-and-a-half. Suddenly, she flopped back onto the pillows and she started the death-rattle. I had seen it before from my work in the hospital.

With that, I turned on my heels and ran up to the kitchen. I said, 'Quick! Gran is dying!' They said, 'No, she's not, didn't she have her dinner.' I said, 'I know she is dying! Come on! She is! She is!' So we went back down to the room and she was gone.

I didn't say anything about what had happened to the rest of the family. I was only in my late teens at the time and I felt I couldn't. I couldn't tell my uncle because he was very strict and would always say, 'I don't want to hear any nonsense talk. Don't be going on with nonsense.' I felt I couldn't tell my mother either because I thought she would tell her brother. I also felt I couldn't tell my own brother. So I just kept quiet and never told anyone for about ten years.

Looking back, I believe that I was brought back for my grandmother's death. I was walking up the road and heading home when I spotted my brother coming towards me. I still remember his words distinctly after I asked him why he was coming back. 'Well, I wasn't, but I just thought I would,' he had said. I don't know what came into his head to go back. It was like a miracle to me. Another person might not see it that way. But I really felt I was brought back and it was a privilege to be there for such a special moment.

I also feel that something really happened at the time that my grandmother died. She looked so happy. Happiness was written all over her. She was smiling. I got the feeling that her arms went into the arms of whoever she was going to. I think that she saw the Blessed Virgin at the end of the bed. I believe she came for her at the hour of her death and took her into her arms and brought her to God.

SEÁN, A PRIEST FROM COUNTY TIPPERARY, recalls the very moving death of his father.

Almost immediately after Christmas 2011, my father, who was 85, took unwell. We were aware of the fact that he had prostate cancer, but we didn't tell him. He was one of those individuals that if you told him, he would die quicker. If you didn't tell him, he would happily trundle on.

Initially, he was hale and hearty and in great form. He was a tall, trim man and looked well. He got on with life and was very active. Although we were hopeful, each time we thought he had got on top of things something else would go wrong. He would get an infection or a cold. Eventually, he was hospitalised and the time came when they told us there were only a couple of days left.

We decided we would like to bring him home. The head nurse in the hospital asked a lady to organise an ambulance. The lady said she would look into it the following day or the day after. The head nurse said, 'Would you do it today as the window is small.' That was the first time I realised that things were going to happen very quickly.

We brought him home and all the family congregated from near and afar. Being the man he was, however, my father held on for a couple of weeks. They were invaluable weeks for everybody, including for me. On one occasion, we were talking and he got upset. He asked me if I would anoint him. It was something I had done many times before with other people, but all of a sudden my own father was asking me for that sacrament. I had a temptation to say, 'I'll get a priest.'

I did it for him and it was a privilege. Afterwards, I looked at him and I asked, 'Are you afraid?' He said he wasn't, although he said he had been afraid at the beginning when he realised he wasn't going to get better. He told me he would cry when we weren't there. 'Right now,' he said, 'all of that is gone. I feel very content. If death happens now, I'll welcome it.' He then suggested that I should say Mass, so all of us gathered in his room and that's what I did.

Following the Mass, after many people had left, he became agitated and he seemed to be looking for something. We said, 'Do you want water?' At this stage, his voice was so weak that he was hard to hear. He shook his head in the negative. 'Do you need to be turned or something?' we asked. Again, he shook his head in the negative. He was sitting propped up with pillows at the time.

He then joined his hands up together in front of him. Mum noticed it first and she asked, 'Do you want us to pray?' His head nodded in the positive. We began some prayers and we felt, 'This is it.' Suddenly, however, he put his hand out to my mother to shake her hand and he said to her, 'I wish you a long life after I go.' He then indicated he wanted to shake hands with us. He did so one after the other. It was our last proper interaction with him in this life.

There was a lull then and we were waiting for the end. But his hand came up again and we thought, 'Maybe he has forgotten he shook hands with us and wants to shake our hands again.' Mum asked him if that's what he wanted. Although he shook her hand once more, he then tapped it and pushed it gently to one side.

The next thing, his hand distinctly started shaking other people's hands in a mid-air motion in what to us was open space. You could clearly see the grasp and the shaking of hands. He was smiling and he looked so happy to be meeting whoever was there. We were looking at one another in confusion and we hadn't a clue what was going on.

After that, he had his two arms out and he was embracing whoever he was meeting. He did this twice. I can remember thinking, 'Some are getting handshakes and smiles, while two are very clearly being embraced.' He then put his left hand out and moved one of the people in the room out of the way to shake hands with someone we couldn't see and who was obviously hidden from his view. Twice he did this, to get the crowd to move back.

My brother looked at me. Although I wasn't sure what to think, I remember saying to myself, 'There are more people in the room than we can see.' Obviously, for my father, the room was packed. Two of those he saw got very distinct embraces and I would love to know who they were. It could have been his mother, who he lost when he was a baby. It could have been his father, who he lost when he was about ten. It could have been anyone, I don't know.

Eventually, he went back to resting and everything eased. The energy of the moment began to slowly dissipate. I remember being upset and going out to get air. I knew this was it, but while I was crying I felt that the whole event had made his dying incredibly more bearable. There was something very consoling in knowing that he had a big crowd waiting for him on the other side.

There was no exchange of words with our father after that. The following day, I helped the nurse to turn him and he was no longer responding. His breathing had changed noticeably. The nurse suggested I call my mum. After I went out to get her, the nurse followed and said to everyone there, 'You had all better come quickly!' We went in and I began the last prayers. After that, he just left us.

I have been at a lot of deathbeds, but if somebody told me the story I'm telling you now I would be savagely sceptical. Yet what happened during that period of time with my father completely changed how I feel about his death. Even at the funeral, there was an enormous calm. It was extraordinary. Everything went from a grief we couldn't avoid to something that was beautifully natural.

Being a priest, I firmly believe there's something there. In my mind, there is no argument. What exactly that something is, and who might be waiting, and what eternity and God might look like, I don't know. But I certainly know that in my father's last hours, he knew more people in the room than we could see. Whatever that means, I have taken huge consolation from it because I saw the look on my father's face. At that time, he was not just ready to die, but he was embracing those on the other side.

MAUREEN, FROM COUNTY LOUTH, remembers her grandmother's death, which occurred when she was just into her teens.

My grandmother had a tough life, running a sweetshop on her own and raising two children. She had lost her husband at an early age. I think my mum was only nine years old when he died. To lose your husband back in those days was very hard. It was difficult raising a son and daughter on your own.

She was a tough lady, but we used to get on very well. I wouldn't take any nonsense from her. She would often be very tough on my mother and make her cry. I would go up to her and give out. She would say, 'I'm sorry, I didn't mean it, come over here and give me a hug.' I think she had time for me.

When I was about 13, my grandmother was dying. She was in her 80s at the time and she was suffering from old age. She had grey hair and wrinkles. She was ailing and I think she had heart trouble. I also think she had a stroke. At this stage, she had been invalided and bedridden for about a year-and-a-half. She couldn't move on her own.

She was in her own bedroom, which was the biggest room upstairs, on the left-hand side of her house. It looked over to the Cooley Mountains. I remember there was a picture up on the wall, displaying the crown of thorns. She used to always wonder would it fall on her, but nobody thought of taking it down. She was lying back in her double bed in this old-fashioned room and she was dying.

We were beside her bed. I was at one side of the bed; my mother was at the other side. My mother was saying the Rosary. There was a neighbour right beside me. As we went through the decades, all I could hear was the sound of my friends playing outside and the only place I wanted to be was with them. I also remember that my mother was crying, with her head down, so she didn't see what happened next.

My grandmother was lying back on the bed with her knees up under her chin. She always used to lie back that way. Suddenly, I could see the bedclothes moving and I could see her knees straightening out. The next thing, my grandmother sat up straight in the bed. She didn't even hold on to the bedclothes as she rose up. She just came bolt upright. I thought, 'My God! What's happening?'

She looked down to the bottom of the bed and this gorgeous smile came to her face. She wasn't a woman for smiling, so it was strange. I had never seen her smile in my life. She stared and she was obviously directing her smile and her greeting to whoever was at the bottom of the bed. There was absolutely no doubt that she had seen something, although there was no person there. I looked in amazement and got the shivers.

It all lasted for a very short time. I put my arm over to her and said, 'Granny, are you alright?' That was all the time it took. With that, she dropped back on to the pillow. I heard the death-rattle and she was gone. After that, I remember the old lady beside me got a hold of my arm and said, 'Her own has come for her. Her husband has arrived.' I had never heard anyone say anything like that before. I looked at her and had to ask her what she meant.

I nursed in England, later on, and I dealt with a lot of people who died. I went to the chaplain there and when I told him about what had happened with my grandmother, he said, 'It was obviously her husband who had come back for her.' I also talked to him about all the other people I was dealing with who were dying. He said, 'Maureen, you are blessed when you are with a person who is dying and breathing their last.'

The chaplain also maintained that your own come for you before you die. I have absolutely no doubt that this is true. I have been around too many dying people, when I worked as a nurse, to doubt it. I think any decent-living person who dies will meet their loved ones again. When the time comes, your own will definitely come for you.

PAULINE, FROM DUBLIN, describes what happened when her sister died in 2000.

My sister Patricia, who I was very close to, moved to New York in the 1960s to work. Eventually, in the early 1990s, she and her husband retired to Las Vegas because they couldn't take any more of the New York winters. She was in her mid-60s at the time. Their children remained in New York.

She was a very good person, not pious, but full of love. I don't think she was the sort of person who went to Mass every Sunday, but she was a believer and a Catholic and very kind. She would never say anything bad about anybody. She had a great generosity and was very 'giving'. People used to say she looked awfully like St. Thérèse and she used to roar laughing when she heard that.

I remember, in June of 2000, she phoned me from Las Vegas and told me she had been vomiting. She mentioned that she and her husband had been out two nights earlier for dinner. I said, 'You must have food poisoning.' She said, 'You are probably right.' I said, 'You should go and see a doctor about it.' So she did, but the doctor wasn't happy and sent her for tests.

In early July, they discovered that she had cancer of the bowel. They told her she was inoperable. Initially, she had to go into hospital for some small surgery. It was there the first strange thing happened. When her husband and daughter went in to visit, she said, 'I had two visitors last night. Why did you send visitors to me?' Her husband said, 'We didn't send any visitors.' She said, 'But they came in and they told me I am going to die in three weeks!'

They asked who the visitors were, but she said she didn't know. She couldn't put names on them; they were strangers. Her daughter then went out to check with the hospital staff about who had come in. They said, 'There was nobody here.

If there was, it would be in her notes.' They also checked with the night nurse and she said there had been no visitors either.

The family then brought her home from the hospital and she was cared for there. She was very ill from then on. She couldn't eat. She would phone me and say, 'I don't want to die.' I would say, 'Don't say that, you'll be alright.' It was very difficult for the family. The children, who were living away from home, took things in relays for the next seven weeks. They helped their father and they looked after her night and day. A few friends helped also.

I remember, during one midweek night in August, her son phoned me. He said, 'If you want to see Mum, you had better come.' The day I arrived was a Friday and she had just gone into a hospice. She was in a private room. It was a beautiful room, with a lovely timber bed, which had to be replaced eventually by a cot. There was a big television in the room and some lovely furniture. It wasn't at all like the sort of hospital room that you would generally see.

We took things in turns. I was with her all night on the Saturday. They were very kind and put in another bed for me. I was also with her on the Sunday. She was completely unconscious, in a coma, from the Sunday morning. She was just lying on the bed, completely motionless, her eyes closed, her head on the pillow, with her hands at the side of the bed and the palms turned up. She was lifeless.

On the Monday, her son and I were both with her. Her husband had gone home for a rest. I was standing on one side of the bed and her son was on the other. She was there with her lifeless hands beside her, completely unconscious, no movement whatsoever, the head sideways. Each of us had a bible. I would say a Psalm and then her son would say another Psalm.

Suddenly, at about 11 o'clock, she lifted up her head from the pillow and her eyes stared up towards the ceiling. Her expression changed. There was no blinking and there was no smile, but her face became alive. There was a look of wonder on her face. Her eyes were big and she was staring in awe. She didn't say anything. This went on for a long time, maybe for a minute or a minute-and-a-half. Her son and I saw it happen and we got a bit of a shock. We were speechless.

Then, very, very slowly, like watching something in slow motion, she took up her right hand and it went from the lifeless position at the side of the bed up to her forehead and she blessed herself. At this stage, I knew she was seeing somebody. She never blinked; she was just looking. Then, very slowly, she took her hand down and closed her eyes and her head went sideways. Not a word was spoken. What happened was so clear and it will never leave me; it will always be with me.

The next thing, the door to her room opened up and a nurse came in. She must have been coming in to check on her. The moment she opened the door, she stepped back. She said, 'Oh, my God! What is going on in this room? There's something beautiful in here.' I was taken aback. I just got my bag and went out. I had to get out, to think straight.

Her son followed me and he asked me, 'What happened?' I said, 'She saw somebody.' He said, 'She did!' He then wondered, 'Would somebody, like her mother, have come for her?' I said, 'Yes.' I certainly knew she saw somebody. What puzzled me, though, was why she would have blessed herself if it was one of her family. That struck me as strange.

She died the very next day, Tuesday, 29 August, aged 72. Afterwards, I came home and I told my family what had happened and we talked about it. Her family also discussed it. But I think they were more interested in her insistence that two strangers had come to see her and told her she would die in three weeks. I suppose they were right to feel that way because she did die around the same time later on. They wondered more about that.

Since then, I feel a great sense of 'spirit' and closeness to God and Mary. It has reinforced my sense of faith. I believe utterly that there is something bigger and greater. I believe there exists a power of great goodness. It has also made me unafraid of death. As I said to one of my sons, 'I have no fear of dying. I won't be afraid.' He said, 'That's because of what happened, isn't it?' I said, 'Yes, it is.'

To me, I believe that it was Christ that was there. I don't know if that was the case, but I think that's why my sister crossed herself. I believe what happened to my sister will also happen to me. I just know somebody will come for me. I hope so anyway. I don't feel I am worthy of it or I don't feel it's my due, but I dearly hope for it and I aspire to it and I hope it happens someday.

HELEN, FROM COUNTY KERRY, recollects what took place when her husband's uncle died in the 1970s.

My husband's uncle was a farmer. He was elderly, in his 80s, and was never married. He just worked away on the farm on his own. He suffered from glaucoma and his sight was very bad. Eventually, he had a stroke. He was in bed and helpless. It must have been difficult for him because he had been a very independent man.

We inherited his farm and we took it over, so we were looking after everything. We were finding it difficult to cope because he was very ill. He had lost most of his bodily functions. My mother-in-law was also in the house at the time. She was in her 70s, but was very independent and well able to fend for herself. We had five children to care for at that stage. In addition, my husband worked the farm. It was a very tough time.

After the stroke, the poor man was confined to bed and was totally out of it. He wasn't aware of what was going on. He was on his last legs. Ours is a one-storey house and he was in a bedroom at the end of a long corridor, looking out on the road. He slept in a double bed. He had the room all to himself, even though at that time we had a lot of children and they had to share.

We thought he would die much earlier than he did. In fact, he lasted about six weeks. At first, he was able to get out of his bed, but as time went on he got worse. We had to look after him all day. My mother-in-law and I would have to lift him up on his bed to feed him or whatever. We had to do everything, including turning him over and back.

I remember we once had to stay up with him all night. We took turns giving him sips of water on the hour, not only all that night but throughout the day, because he had become dehydrated. The doctor had advised us to do that. The priest eventually had to come and anoint him. He was dying.

There was one day, shortly before he died, which was pretty much no different from any other. He was lying on his back, on his bed, with pillows behind him. I was standing on one side of the bed and my mother-in-law was on the other side. We were looking after him.

Suddenly, he made an almighty effort and straightened himself up on his own. He more or less pulled himself up in the bed. He looked towards the end of the bed and he called out, 'Jim! Jim!' and 'Kate! Kate!' Jim and Kate were his brother and sister and they were dead for several years. They were the only members of the family who had died at that stage.

There was a look of pure joy and delight on his face. You could see his face lighting up and it was totally animated. It was clear that he was seeing people and he was so pleased to see them. He no longer noticed us and it was as if we weren't there at all.

The look was the sort that you would expect from a person who was meeting someone they hadn't seen for years. You can imagine how delighted they would be if the unexpected visitor was suddenly standing at their door. That's how happy he was.

The whole thing lasted for only a minute or two. He then just lay down and closed his eyes and nothing more was said. He never spoke to us about what had happened. Not long afterwards, he died.

I remember the day that he died. It was the Feast of the Assumption and I was at Mass. My husband was with him. My mother-in-law was with him, too. He simply passed away very peacefully. I was arriving from Mass and my husband was there saying, 'Come on! Quick!' I was talking to one of the neighbours and wondering what the worry was. When I got back to the gate, my husband told me, 'Tom has just died!'

I wasn't at all surprised by what had happened. I had heard of this sort of thing before. We live in a rural area and I had often come across it. As a result, I always believed that when death was near, our own people would come and help us across the divide to the other side. I'm still sure of that.

I think that's what happened with Tom. I believe he joined the rest of the family who were already gone. I really believe that's what it was. His brother and sister came for him, probably to help him and to reassure him that he was safe. They had both been close to him, even though he was a bachelor and very independent. He had been good to his

42

sister Kate and was very fond of her. He had also kept in touch with his brother Jim, who had gone to America and never returned.

It wasn't the only time I had a strange experience. Years before, when that same brother Jim died in America, I remember I was in the house with my mother-in-law and father-in-law. I was a new bride at the time and I was preparing the supper and setting the table. I suddenly looked towards the room door and saw somebody big, with light clothes.

At the time, I shook my head and was worried that my mother-in-law and father-in-law had seen me because they might think they were getting somebody who was crazy. I said, 'I'd better pull myself together or they will think I am daft.' However, a letter arrived soon afterwards informing us that Jim had passed away in America. The letter mentioned the day he had died and that was the day I had seen the figure by the door.

What happened, in both cases, proves to me that there is another dimension and that we have an immortal soul. That soul will never die, but is there forever and will go on to infinity. Eventually, please God, we will end up in his presence for all eternity and we will be in a very joyful place. That's what we are told, 'Eye hath not seen, nor ear heard, neither have entered into the heart of man, the things which God hath prepared for them that love him.'

DIARMAID, FROM COUNTY CORK, has direct and indirect knowledge of many people's deathbed visions. He begins with the death of his father in 1997.

My father died a day or two before his seventy-first birthday. He had emphysema and had been very sick for a while. His illness had gone on for just over two years. He was a heavy smoker, although he gave up the cigarettes when he knew he was dying. At the end, he was on oxygen and he was aware he was going.

Things got very bad around the Christmas of 1996. He was very breathless. By that stage, not only could he not go to Mass, as he used to, but he couldn't even walk across the street. He had the oxygen and inhalers beside him. We knew the end was coming, although we didn't think it was going to be so fast. He died in January 1997.

A day or two before he died, he asked me to shave him. I did the shave in his bedroom. He half sat up in the bed. It was a wet shave and he was just sitting there. I could hear the death-rattle in his chest. He started saying to me, 'I wish you God's blessing.' He then said that he had been visited by his brother-in-law, my uncle.

He also said, 'All the lovely young people!' The thing I remember about him saying 'All the lovely young people!' to me was the way he was staring at the same time. It was as if he was looking into my eyes but beyond me. He said the same thing to my sister, 'All the lovely young people!' at a different time. I was surprised and knew it was a sure sign that something was happening. He eventually slipped into a coma and died fast enough.

I had seen something similar before with my wife's uncle, who had died back in 1989. He was an unmarried man and my wife was caring for him before his death. He had been unwell and bedridden for months. I think he had cancer and he wasn't able to swallow in the end. We had been told he would die the previous Christmas, but he held out until St. Patrick's Day.

A day or two before he died, he started to look around the bedroom and, reaching out his hand, said, 'All the people, where are they all going?' In addition, he called out the names of his brother and sister, who had predeceased him. He, again, was staring into the far distance as he said each of these things.

He also said, over and over, 'Palms, palms, everywhere!' Strangely, he was buried on Palm Sunday and his coffin was covered in palms. That was the first time I came across this sort of thing, so when I heard my father all those years later, I wasn't that surprised. I said, 'I've seen this before.'

There's another man I know of, who had suffered a heart attack but was back to full health and was not expected to die. A year or two after his heart attack, he was sitting at home one evening with his wife and son-in-law and daughter-in-law. They were chatting away. Suddenly, he stood up and asked his son-in-law to walk with him to the front door. He just said, 'Come to the door with me.'

They opened the door and looked out into the yard. He then asked, pointing with his forefinger, 'Who is he?' The son-in-law looked and could see nothing, but he knew straight away that something was very wrong. He had an immediate sixth sense. So they walked back into the living-room, where the man collapsed and died suddenly on the floor. He had known somebody was outside for him, but who it was I don't know.

Eventually, my wife died at the age of 55. She suffered a major stroke to the stem of her brain, leaving her paralysed and speechless for over six months. However, for the greater part of that time, although she was aware of what was happening, she could only communicate by looking up for a 'yes' and down for a 'no'.

Before she died, she used to look beyond me, over my shoulder. On a few occasions, she opened her eyes and looked as if she was seeing something that surprised her. She would roll around in the bed and look over the bed as if she was seeing something in the beyond. I think it was her people coming for her.

We all have our opinions as to what goes on. I definitely believe, from everything I have witnessed, that they are not hallucinations, although sceptics and non-believers might think they are. The people that I have seen or that I know of weren't feverish either. Instead, I have faith and I believe what happens has something to do with an afterlife.

I really don't know what the reference my father made to 'all the young people' is about. In my opinion, I think it means that we're all going to look transfigured, different or young after we pass away. I think it's probably that our family and friends and many more come to us looking that way. But I really don't know.

However, I think that what happened to my father and all the others will also happen to me when I die. I would expect to see my wife again and my parents and whoever else, including Christ himself. The Lord is the master of all these things and whoever we see will be whoever he designs. All will eventually be revealed.

MARY, FROM COUNTY KILDARE, explains what occurred shortly before her husband's death from cancer.

Back in 2002, my husband Frank was diagnosed with non-Hodgkin's lymphoma. I was stunned and I couldn't speak when I heard it. Frank asked the doctor was it treatable. 'It's very treatable,' he was told. That was the start. He went through huge chemotherapy, which was very aggressive, beginning in May of that year. He lost his hair and had the usual side-effects.

We had a lot of things to deal with that year. Frank got septicaemia and his mother died. He later told me that, just after his mother died, he woke up one morning and said to himself, 'My mother is dead and I'm battling cancer. How am I going to face all of this?' As he said this to himself, it was like his mother had put her arms around him and he felt a weight lifting from his head to his feet. From then on, he never looked back.

He went through the chemotherapy and the cancer went into remission. He was back working in 2003. Everything was perfect. His job was going well. However, at Christmas 2007, Frank became unwell again. We were both involved in the church choir and he was to sing 'O Holy Night'. He was a fabulous tenor singer, with the voice of an angel, but he complained about his throat being sore. He asked me to ring and say he couldn't do it.

When he went to see his consultant, in early March, it turned out that the cancer had actually spread to his throat. It had come back with aggression. He had chemotherapy and radiotherapy. He experienced weight loss. We went away on holidays. Unfortunately, the treatment didn't work and he died the following August.

I remember, in the August, we dropped Frank up to the hospital in Dublin on a Wednesday. He was having his scans on a Thursday. We had never spoken about death or dying. Nor had we spoken about it with the consultant. However, when I went up on the Friday, there was a message saying that the consultant wanted to see me. I went to him, he sat me down and he said, 'Frank has three to four days to live.' He said the scans were shocking. I was devastated.

I went back up to Frank, who was propped up in his hospital bed. My heart was breaking, knowing what I knew. I couldn't say to him, 'Frank, I've got terrible news. You are dying.' He didn't say it to me either. I just shaved him and asked him, 'How are you?' He said, 'I'm tired.' He was weak. Apparently, the cancer had been going right through him in the previous five weeks.

Everything happened so quickly after that. The following day, the Saturday, my youngest son flew back from holidays and arrived at the hospital. At this stage, Frank was sleeping and waking and showing no interest. However, when our son came in, Frank lit up and said, 'Where are you coming from?' Our son replied, 'I'm back from my holidays. How are you?' 'I'm OK,' Frank said. They were his last words. Later that day, he went into a deep sleep.

He didn't die until the next Tuesday morning. However, a strange thing happened on the Sunday. We were all sitting around the bed. I was on Frank's left. Suddenly, he raised his left arm and hand as if he was reaching out to somebody. It was like as if somebody was waiting to catch his hand and he was reaching out to them, as if he was responding to someone who was saying, 'Give me your hand!'

At first, I thought he was trying to reach out to us or to find us. I said to him, 'Frank, I'm here. We're all here with you.' Still, however, he kept reaching out. There was no body movement; he would just raise his left arm and hand. He did it again and again. I was holding and squeezing his hand, but he would just lift it up in the air and reach out.

At this stage, he was lying back with two or three pillows behind him. His eyes were closed and he was breathing heavily. It was strange that it was his left hand he was raising because he wasn't left-handed. But I knew that he was reaching out. This continued for some time, probably up until Monday evening. It was only afterwards that I began to piece together what he had done.

I had never seen anybody die. My father and mother had already died, but I wasn't living at home at that stage and didn't witness their deaths. Frank was the first I ever saw. I was worried that he would be distressed. I even remember saying to the priest, 'Would you please pray to God to take Frank and not let us sit and have to look at him suffering.' He said, 'Mary, it doesn't work that way. When God wants him, he will take him.'

It didn't happen like I had feared at all. It was totally the opposite. There was a great sense of peace. Frank wasn't tormented. He also wasn't agitated. I couldn't believe how peaceful he was. He was just in that deep sleep. All we did was keep the candles lighting. We kept the prayers going. His breathing got shallower and shallower and subsided. I think he was well on his way to wherever he was going.

We then moved into the Tuesday morning, 5 August 2008, and it was spilling rain even though it was August. We all said the Rosary around the bed. At that time, Frank was no longer raising his hand. Then, as we just finished the Rosary, at 7.25 in the morning, Frank took his last breath. The priest looked at me and said, 'Mary, he's gone.' None of us around the bed made a move. We just sat there. We didn't scream or shout or cry. It was like blowing out a candle. There was no struggle or fight. It was such a peaceful death.

His death was such a shame. He was only 63. We were soul mates, a team. He was an outdoor person and a worker and he worked hard. He was a people's person. Everybody loved him. He had a great sense of humour and a smile you would kill for. He wasn't one to complain or talk about his troubles.

But we never die and our memories live on long after we pass away. Today, I sit here in the living-room, with a picture of Frank on the mantelpiece and a candle lit. Every bit of him is still in the house. It's like he's never left, but I just can't see him. I still feel his presence. He was my rock and he still is.

Looking back, I definitely know that Frank was reaching out and he wasn't reaching out to us. I know that he had been very close to his parents, who were both dead. They had died at an old age. His mum had been the last to pass away and he could have been reaching out to her. Or he could have been reaching out to his father. He had been a very good son to his parents; he was unreal, a special man. I think they were coming for him, no doubt.

I believe there is a life hereafter and I believe there is a superior being. I believe the superior being is working with those of us who struggle with bad health. I also believe that dead relatives will come to meet us when we are dying. It's like what we were taught when we were growing up: that everyone will meet again. I think there is no doubt about that. No one could convince me otherwise.

PHIL, FROM COUNTY WATERFORD, remembers the deathbed vision experienced by her dying aunt.

My aunt was in her early 90s when she died. She had reared three daughters, but one was dead. She had also reared a son. Her husband had passed away many years before her. She was a very good woman, very religious and was always a kind person. When you'd call in to her, you'd always have to have the tea. She was a real countrywoman.

In her early years, she used to do a little bit of work for a farmer down the road, but the payment then was just a bottle of milk. They were hard and tough times. Otherwise, she reared her children and she always went out of her way to look after our family, too. We went to the same school and we'd always call up at lunchtime and we'd have our lunch in their house. We'd also call up early in the morning to walk down to school with her family. I suppose we really grew up together.

As she got older, she had to be looked after by one of her daughters. The daughter minded her at home. Sometimes, it was thought that she had a bit of dementia, but she really hadn't. She also wasn't on medication, except maybe a little bit for the swelling of her legs. It was only in the last three weeks that she was confined to bed. Before that, she would get up every day. She was very 'with it'.

One afternoon, around three or four o'clock, I was with her. Her daughter was there as well. So was a priest. She was getting feeble at this stage and her body was weak. The priest was just leaving and her daughter was looking after him, letting him out. I was left with her in the room. It was then that I saw her hearing and speaking to somebody else.

She was propped up against pillows in the bed. The next thing, she looked straight across from her, staring upwards towards the ceiling or the top of the wall. Her mouth and lips were moving as if she was talking to somebody and saying something to them. It looked like she was having a conversation. She wasn't aware of anybody else in the room, only what she saw. Her hands didn't move. What she saw took all her attention.

I looked up to see what she was looking at, but there was nothing there. Yet I knew something important was going on, that she was definitely seeing somebody and was talking to them. It looked like others were welcoming her to the other side and that she knew them. It looked like they were coming for her and that she was seeing those that had gone before. I was sure something was going on. She died shortly afterwards. Her death was very peaceful.

I've heard of other people having this sort of experience. When my first cousin was only two years of age, he got a dreadful flu. He was a real little angel, with curly blond hair. He was lying on the sofa and he just raised himself up, stretched out his arms and gave a big smile as if somebody was going to take him into their arms. His mother saw this happen. There was nobody else there, nobody standing in front of him. His mother felt they were coming for him. He was a lovely little fellow and too good for this world. He died a short time later.

I believe that all those who have gone before come to meet us and they will be there when we go to the other side. I suppose it comes from my faith, but I know it happens in real life as well. I've also heard other people talk about these sort of stories. Older people, in particular, talk about them. So I do believe these things happen and that old family and friends will be there to welcome us across. And I definitely believe that both my aunt and little cousin were being met by somebody shortly before they died.

CLARE, FROM DUBLIN, recalls her mother's communications with the 'Master' close to the time of her death.

My mother was born in 1906. She was aged ten at the time of the uprising in 1916. She had clear recollections of that. Her uncle was in Kilmainham Gaol for his part in the event. She remembered her mother walking to Kilmainham with a baby in the pram, bringing a jug of soup wrapped in a towel to keep it warm, up to my uncle. She also remembered the Civil War. She came from a different era.

As a person, she possessed a wicked sense of humour, was extremely imaginative and very gentle as well. She raised four children and also had many grandchildren. They all loved her. My father loved her, too. People weren't very demonstrative in those days. However, I still have a clear picture of my father arriving home and my mother standing at the cooker. He walked in and put his hand on her back and said, 'I'm home, woman.' That was his way of being affectionate.

Ultimately, my mother suffered from bad health. She and my dad had been smokers. There was always a packet of cigarettes knocking around. My father literally killed himself by smoking; he died early from emphysema. She had given up cigarettes, but the damage was done to her circulation. I remember her saying to me one morning, 'I have an awful pain in my foot.' I looked and her little toe was blue. She had to have surgery to correct the circulation to her feet. She also had arthritis and was in constant pain.

Eventually, in 1987, at almost 81 years of age, she was diagnosed as having myeloma, which is cancer of the bone marrow. She got weaker and weaker. The doctor told us, 'She's not going to live long.' She remained at home in the house from then until she died. We had a rota of people to look after her. The family were brilliant.

The night before she passed away, my brother decided to stay with her. She was getting quite weak at this stage. She was sleeping and waking and sleeping again. At breakfast, my brother said, 'She was talking through the night.' I asked him who she was talking to. He said she was talking to the 'Master.' I wondered was it a schoolmaster. He said, 'No, she was just talking quietly and every now and then I would hear, "Yes, Master! Yes, Master!"'

She said the same thing again on the following day, which was the day she died. The room has a window on what was her right-hand side as she lay in the bed. There's a little bit of a wall and then there's the end-wall of the room. We had her propped up with pillows in her bed.

She wasn't talking to us at the time. Instead, she kept looking into the corner down by the end-wall. Every now and then, this little smile would appear on her face. She would open her eyes and turn her head to look into the corner. She would lift her hand as if she was reaching out and she would say, 'Master!'

I felt I should ring for our local priest. Down he came and he sat down. All my family were praying beside my mother. He said to me at one stage, 'There is a most extraordinary atmosphere in this house.' He later left. Shortly afterwards, my mother looked over into the corner of the bedroom, way beyond us all. She smiled and said, 'Master!' Her breathing then just quietly stopped and she was gone.

I don't think we were surprised by what we saw. As soon as we had our First Communion, our father brought us to daily Mass. Jesus and God and religion and the faith and the Rosary were all part of our lives. Our faith was important to us. It was therefore no surprise that our mother should be in communion with God, although I wondered why it wasn't our father who had come to her. I believed it was God she was talking to.

I remember a priest once talked to a group I was part of about Mass. He talked about the Consecration, when Jesus is there and there's the presence of the choirs of angels and the saints. He talked about the wonder that it is. He also said that all our friends and loved ones that are gone before us are there, too.

I also believe in that. I am convinced that our deceased relatives are never far away. When we die, I believe they will be there. There will be familiar people around. I firmly expect my mother and father will be very close, along with other people I knew. I am convinced of that.

MARGARET, FROM COUNTY CORK, explains what her mother-in-law saw shortly before her death.

My mother-in-law died in 2002. She lived with us here in the house. She had done so all her life. She died in our house, too. She hated hospitals and wanted to keep away from them. It was probably because her husband had died in one when he was very young. She did go into hospital for a few medical procedures, like a knee operation, but she really did not want to die there. Her wish was to die at home.

She was 97 years of age when she died. She had her senses about her right up to that time. She was talking to the doctor an hour before she passed away. She was totally 'with it'. At the time, she was in her own bedroom, which she had been living in for years and years. She had been weak for some time, but she was still able to talk.

We knew she wasn't well. The doctor had come to her a couple of times and she had told us that her pulse and her heartbeat had gone very weak and that she wouldn't last long. About 11 or 12 of us had come to the house for her last hours. We were in the bedroom with her. There were brothers and sisters, husbands and wives and some neighbours. We were all saying the Rosary around the bed.

She was propped up in the bed and sleeping away. She would occasionally open her eyes. She was half following us and trying to keep up with the Rosary prayers. Suddenly, she moved forward from the pillows. She didn't reach out her hands, but she couldn't because she had a Rosary beads in them and her hands were joined.

As she leaned forward in the bed, she said, 'Hannah Dan!' The woman she was referring to was called Hannah Dan. She was called Hannah Dan to distinguish her from Hannah Jack and others called Hannah in the locality. Most were called after their fathers. Hannah's father was named Dan. Hannah Dan had been dead for years, probably even before my mother-in-law got married.

My mother-in-law had known Hannah Dan when she was growing up. She would always talk about her. They were old friends and neighbours living next door to each other. My mother-in-law's mother had passed away when she was young. She was having another baby, I think, when she got kidney failure and died. My mother-in-law was only four years of age at the time.

Hannah Dan, who had a family of her own, had taken my mother-in-law under her wing. She had protected her as a child. When the daffodils would blossom, she would always say to us about Hannah Dan taking her out collecting them. She would talk about how they would look for primroses or pick blackberries together, all the simple things they would do. They had happy times together.

She had a great smile on her face as she said the name. She was so pleased. Her face lit up as it would do if you saw a friend you hadn't seen for a long time. There was pure joy written all over her and she looked so happy and surreal. You would know she had just seen someone. She was so delighted. She died about 15 minutes later.

We were all pleased for my mother-in-law having seen what she saw. We were a little surprised because she had buried her husband 50 years ago and we all thought how she would be meeting him. He had died young. We were always saying someone would be waiting for her and we thought it would be her husband. Instead, we all said, 'My God! It's Hannah Dan she has met!' Everyone knew exactly who she was talking about.

My sister-in-law experienced something similar herself. She was a nurse. One day, she was caring for a patient who was dying in a private room. She knew the family well. As she came out the door of the room, she sensed someone else was going in. She thought it was the mother of the woman in the room who was arriving. She recognised the voice of the mother, who was dead. But she couldn't see anyone. It really struck her. She wondered was she hallucinating. The woman in the room was dead within half an hour.

I really think people come to meet you when you die. I know my father's mother called out the name of an aunt, not her mother or father. My mother would always talk about how someone had come to help her and to take her away. Other people used to talk about it as well. In particular, the old people used always say that somebody would be waiting for you and that someone would come for you to help you over. I, too, believe these things happen. Having seen it for myself, I know it is real.

MARION, FROM COUNTY OFFALY, describes what happened shortly before the death of her mother in April 2002.

My mother was aged 87 when she died. She had chronic emphysema, so her breathing wasn't great. She had been a smoker and it had affected her badly. She was staying in our house and she was sleeping in the sitting-room because she couldn't manage the stairs. She slept in a single bed, which was in one corner of the room.

She loved staying with us, especially being with the kids. They got on brilliantly. She was, however, very unwell not just with the emphysema but with Alzheimer's and old age. She was afraid of dying and of being on her own, so I had to stay with her, sleeping on a mattress for two years.

The day that I realised she was really bad was when she couldn't swallow her antibiotics. I panicked and I went around to the chemist. I asked, 'Is there a powder or liquid form for this?' I remember that my husband followed me around. When I saw him, I just broke out crying and said, 'She's dying!' We got the antibiotics and went home.

Back home, my mother wanted to get out of bed. She did so and she sat on the chair. It was about one o'clock or two o'clock in the afternoon. I remember she sat down and cuddled up to me. I put my arm around her, like she was a child. She sat there for maybe 20 minutes and then she got tired. She decided to get back into bed and I propped her up.

I asked her if she wanted to say some prayers. She found it hard to speak because of the emphysema; she was very short of breath. But she loved the Rosary and with the Hail Marys she was able to do them with pauses and without stressful breathing, so that's what we said. Afterwards, I went out to the kitchen and my husband stayed to keep an eye on her. When I came back in, I asked him, 'How is she?' He said, 'She's fine, she's so relaxed and calm and peaceful.'

As I sat down beside her, I looked and saw that she had a smile on her face. It was a smile like no other smile. The smile was in her eyes as well. Her face shone in the way that a face would shine when someone is really happy. It was as if a beam of light was coming across it. She was also very slowly lifting up her hand as if she was pointing to something. She was pointing to somewhere beyond where we were.

Her face was serene and she had a fixed, faraway look. It wasn't like she was staring; the look was a bit more subtle. She looked so pleased, whatever it was that she saw. Her look was very, very strange, especially when someone is as sick as she was. When you are sick, your eyes don't stay fixed like hers. They get tired and they droop, but hers didn't. She stayed like that for maybe a minute.

I gestured to my husband, questioning if he could see what I just saw. He could. There was a moment of silent recognition between us. Although we both saw the moment of intense joy, we didn't break the spell. We both stayed absolutely still. It was her moment.

It was clear to us that something was going on that we

couldn't put our finger on or that we couldn't describe. It was as if something was happening within her person. I felt that we couldn't draw her out of it and couldn't break it. It was like there was a wall around her and we shouldn't interfere with her space.

She then put her hand down, although her eyes stayed fixed. After that, everything became very serene. She no longer seemed afraid of dying. She was at peace. I think it was then that we accepted she was dying and we were in the last few stages. We watched her after that and I sat with her. Although it happened once more about an hour or so later, where she looked beyond her realm, it wasn't as intense as before.

She died that night. She was in bed and very frail at that point. I knew she wanted to hold my hand, but I didn't want her to get cold so I put my hand under the sheet. I remember she muttered to me, 'Marion, there's money in the wardrobe. I'd like you to have something.' She didn't really have much money, but she was trying to look after me. I think it was her way of saying thanks.

She slowly passed away. I said the Rosary, but she couldn't say it with me. I heard the death-rattle. I wondered was it the emphysema, but it was different to what I had heard before. Eventually, I got tired and fell asleep on the mattress. When I woke up, at about 6.30 or seven in the morning, she was gone. I think it was the silence that woke me.

Initially, I felt annoyed because I hadn't been awake with her as she had passed away. However, some people say that the dying pick their moment and maybe she didn't want me to be there; maybe she was happy for me to be asleep. I don't think I cried. I was really happy for her, especially after what had taken place. I was very comforted by the sense of peace.

The way we later interpreted what had happened was that

there was certainly something she saw and wanted to get to, possibly the light. She had no problem going there. She was also letting go, especially letting go of the fear. She knew she was on a journey. She was going home and she was content to go there.

I will never forget the beautiful smile on her face. Because one of my brothers lived in America and had to come home, she had to be embalmed. When she was embalmed, the smile wasn't the same. It wasn't at all the beautiful, happy smile with the sense of acceptance that was on her face after she looked beyond to wherever she was going.

What occurred gave me great spiritual peace. I knew my mother was at peace and I now know I will be with her one day and at peace, too. If I died tomorrow, it wouldn't matter to me. It has taken all the fear away. The thought of dying under a bus doesn't worry me. I really mean that. I mean it because, just like my mother, I would be going home.

I feel the same way about my children. I feel that they are on loan. They don't belong to me; instead, I'm here to look after them and mind them and love them, which I do dearly. But the day might come when someone will knock on my door and say that one of them has passed on. While I would be very upset and very sad, I would know they will be safe. I would know that because they would be going home, too. My mother's death has confirmed that for me.

MAY, FROM COUNTY MEATH, recollects what occurred at a neighbour's deathbed many decades ago.

About 40 years ago, in the early 1970s, we lived in Cork. We lived there for about four years. I had this friend, a neighbour, who lived close by. She lived with her husband in a bungalow. They were very simple people, had no family and were old, well into their 70s or their 80s. However, the two of them were very independent and had promised that they would never send each other to a nursing home after they got old or unwell.

Unfortunately, the husband became very ill. I think it was cancer. He was really bad. Taking care of him was tough going, as there was just the two of them. He also wasn't really able to communicate. I was helping out, as I knew them fairly well. I did whatever I could, giving him drinks or whatever.

Early one morning, we were both with him in the bedroom in their bungalow. He was lying in his bed, feeling unwell, and would have been groaning and calling out to his wife at that stage. I had been there for the whole night into the early hours of the morning. I was just sitting there.

Suddenly, he seemed to shoot up in the bed. He became animated. His whole face lit up and became luminous, just like the face of a saint. His countenance changed from that of a sick man and he became much brighter. He had this loving expression on him.

Immediately, on sitting up, he looked down to the end of the bed and said, 'Jesus!' He said it just once and he said it in a very loving way. He was staring straight ahead. He really looked as if he saw Our Lord. He said nothing else and there was no interaction with us. The whole thing lasted for about a minute and he then lay back down again.

I didn't react or say anything or do anything. I think I'm one of those stoic people. I didn't talk about it with his wife. In fact, I don't even know if she noticed it or registered it, as she wasn't in great health herself. Maybe she just didn't realise what was going on.

That had happened at about seven or eight o'clock in the morning. I rang the doctor soon after. Eventually, at about nine o'clock, they took him into hospital. We travelled after the ambulance to accompany him. He didn't say much other than to speak briefly to his wife. All he said was, 'You're Ida,' which was her name.

We then came home because they had him all wired up and they were taking X-rays. We had only arrived in when we got word that he was dead. He had died at about 11 o'clock, just hours after the vision at the bottom of the bed.

It was a wonderful experience for me. It was amazing to see the life in his face. It was so illuminated, as if Our Lord had just appeared to him. It was clear that he had seen him. It had to have been that, the way his whole countenance shone. It was strange to think of it. I thought to myself, 'He must have been such a good man.'

A similar thing happened on another occasion. This was in the mid-2000s or thereabouts. The father of a friend of mine was a very holy man and very religious. Unfortunately, he too got cancer and was very unwell. My friend and her sister were with him at his hospital bedside. He was just lying there in his bed.

He suddenly said, 'She's very beautiful, isn't she?' He was looking down to the bottom of the bed. They said, 'Who are you talking about?' He said, 'Our Mother, of course!' They knew it was Our Lady he was referring to. He saw her there at the end of the bed. The whole thing meant so much to the daughters. It also reinforced things for me.

I think about what happened down in Cork occasionally, although I never told anyone at the time, not even my husband. I have only said it to the odd person since. Yet, to me, what occurred was a real, heavenly experience. And the memory of it has registered with me and stayed with me all this time, even though it happened 40 years ago.

What took place has helped convince me that there is something else there. I have a good faith anyway, but it has probably reinforced that. It has revealed to me that God is there, that Jesus is there and it probably brought my religious conviction alive for me. There are so many proofs everywhere, but we don't tend to talk about them and we often don't realise what they are. Yet they are there, and if we look for them, these proofs can tell us a lot about life after death.

MÁIRÉAD, FROM LIMERICK, says that her sister-in-law spoke of a 'crowded room' shortly before she died.

My sister-in-law had been in perfect health all her life. She was a nurse in the UK and worked hard. She looked very well. She had been to Ireland not long before she died and I never saw her looking so healthy. She was a very solid, bright woman. She was also a lovely person, very real, and I liked her very much.

One day, a few months after returning to the UK, she got a little pain in the lower back. She said she would rest. She took a week off work and decided she would paint a room in the house. It was amazing she took the time off because it wasn't really like her to do that. Unfortunately, although she bought the paint, she never got to use it and she never painted the room.

Very quickly, the pain got worse and they had to call the doctor. He didn't make too much of it; he thought it was shingles. There also was the possibility it might have been pain from lifting things because she was in that kind of work. Soon, however, it got worse. In the night, it was really affecting her. She was rolling around in agony. She told my brother that he would end up having to carry her to the hospital if he didn't get her in straight away.

He decided to bring her in. When she went for an X-ray, they all just looked at one another. There were big clouds everywhere on the X-ray scan. They diagnosed her as having cancer of the ovaries and it had moved fast. Apparently, that particular cancer is hard to detect. They told her she had eight weeks and that she wasn't going to come out of it. She literally went from perfect to being given eight weeks to live.

They admitted her and she never got out of the hospital again. From then on, she went to hell and back. They did their best for her and helped her as best they could, but the cancer hadn't been caught early enough. They didn't treat it because it had spread so far, so fast. I couldn't believe it. It came as a big shock. She had only just been home and she was grand.

After that, everything went bad rapidly. My brother took time off. He brought her out once or twice, but he had to bring her back very fast as she was that bad and suffering. She would say, 'If there is anyone suffering in the world today as much as this, I'd love to meet them.' She was in a lot of pain. My brother went berserk. They had no children and he knew he was going to be lonely without her. He was only the same age as her.

One day, she was in her hospital bed and my brother was there, too. They didn't know it was the end, although they knew it was close. He had spent all day beside her. At one stage, he felt he had to go to the toilet. The toilet was nearby, but outside the room. Although he badly needed to go, he decided to stay with her. Eventually, she said, 'You can go now because the room is full of people! They're all here for me!'

A smile came on her face. He saw nobody else in the room, so he said, 'I'll be back in a second.' He then stepped outside to go to the toilet. When he came back, she was gone. She had died aged 44. Those were her last words: 'You can go now because the room is full of people! They're all here for me!'

My brother was very annoyed. He was raging that he had missed her last moments. He hadn't been far, just seconds away. Later, he told me about what had happened, including what his wife had said and that he had seen nobody in the room. I had never heard of anything like that before. He was very upset and I'm sure her words will stick in his mind forever.

I believe she saw her dead relatives. She must have known who they were and felt very comfortable with them as she was smiling. They were probably her people, although we don't know. I think she had lost two sisters and maybe her parents, not to mention all those who disappear out of your life every day including neighbours and grandparents and others you have known. But she never mentioned who they were, just that the room was full.

Although I accept that she was dying, I believe she wasn't hallucinating. She was a solid person. Not only was she a nurse, but she had done psychiatric nursing as well. So I believe her relatives were undoubtedly there. Maybe these friends and relatives are always there, but we haven't the eye to see. Maybe they are always around, but we just can't see them.

Maybe we only see them as we die and they help take us to the other side or whatever the next place is. I think there are many rooms for us where we will go, and our dead friends and families will be guiding us and leading us and preparing us for our journey there. I used always like the song about seeing people 'across a crowded room,' but that concerned the living. I never realised that it could also be a 'crowded room' when you die.

MARGARET, FROM COUNTY LONGFORD, outlines what took place when a neighbour died in January 1974.

There was a lovely old man who lived beside us in County Longford. He lived in a one-bedroom house and owned a couple of small fields. He was aged 73 when I was born. I gravitated to him and he looked after me a lot. He was a wonderful person, an absolute gentleman, a good soul and a really happy man. He couldn't read, but he could say the Scripture from Mass. He taught me lots of things and told me lots of stories. He helped prepare me for Communion and Confirmation. He was very good to me.

When he was in his 90s, he got sick. He was dying of old age. We took him into our home to look after him. We brought over his cat, too, to make sure that he was very comfortable and happy. I was aged 17 at that stage and I looked after him a lot of the time. I used to read to him as I sat on the side of his bed. I never minded because he was such a lovely man.

One day, I went into his room and I was about to sit down on the side of his bed. 'Don't sit on Mary! Don't sit on her!' he suddenly said. I couldn't see anybody, so I said, 'Who's Mary?' 'She's my sister, who died when she was seven. I know you can't see her, but I can. She has never got old and she has come for me. She is here with me. Don't sit on her!' he replied.

'I can't see her,' I said to him. He said, 'I know, but don't sit there!' He then sort of gently pushed me down a little bit on the bed, away from where he knew Mary was, and I was happy with that. I moved down and read the book I had with me. I remember I was reading to him about Michael Collins.

I could see that he meant what he said. He was totally

genuine. He wasn't hallucinating or raving or anything else. He was fully conscious about what was happening. He even knew that there was no way I could see her. He hadn't been rambling or going on about strange things as people might do when they are ill or dying. He wasn't imagining things.

It seems that Mary had died when she was seven from TB or some other illness that children died from way back then. He seemed delighted to know she was there. He was very happy and pleased that she had come. And you could see that he knew perfectly well that he was the only person who could see her. That was the only time he told me about Mary or mentioned that she was there.

He died about a week after that. Up to the time he passed away, everything was very quiet and peaceful. He had no worries about dying. He had all the sacraments. A doctor was called, just to check on him, not to do anything as nothing could be done. The doctor said to him, 'You've had a great life.' He replied, 'I have had a great life and I'm dying like a king.'

I believe his sister Mary came to him as he was dying. Although he also had a brother who had died, it was only Mary he mentioned. He never referred to his parents either, who were dead, nor to an aunt. That fascinated me because Mary was only seven when she had passed away. She must have died 90 years earlier, which was such a long time beforehand.

To me, it was wonderful to think that after all that length of time she would remember him. For the rest of us, even after a short time, we forget most of the people we have known. But Mary was there as he was dying and he knew her and recognised her. She was the same as when she left; she never got old. And she came for her brother, no doubt saying, 'Don't worry, I'm here!' I thought it was lovely.

ELIZABETH, FROM COUNTY CORK, describes what took place when her sister died.

Some years ago, I lost a well-beloved sister to a malignant tumour. It was a tumour in the stomach, I think. There was no cure for it. The medical people couldn't do much more than they had done. The family also didn't want to put her through any unnecessary surgery or anything else. She was into her 80s at that stage.

My sister had become incapacitated with the passage of time and was in a lovely nursing home, where she got the best of care. Her immediate family looked after her a lot and were extremely supportive and loving. I used to go visit her, too, because I was the freest to do so. I would sit with her and be there beside her.

She was in good enough shape, although sometimes she didn't realise where she was. Occasionally, she got confused. Towards the end, she had great difficulty breathing and she was refusing to die. The doctor warned me that death was coming. I presume that she knew what was coming, too, although I am not sure if they had told her everything. But she certainly clung on to life.

I was in my nephew's house the evening she passed away and having supper there. He and his wife had been extremely good to my sister, as had all their family, and had given her very loving attention. My nephew was exhausted as a result. He said, 'I'm extremely tired, so I'm just going to lie on my bed and have a rest and I'll join you later at the nursing home.'

His wife and I headed off to the nursing home and I remember saying, 'God rest us tonight!' I hardly knew why I was saying it. I'm a bit cowardly in the face of death – I suppose many people are – so initially I almost refused to go into her room. My niece, who was there, didn't want to go in either. There were four other members of the family in the room.

The medical staff seemed to have gone off the scene and disappeared. They had withdrawn very quietly. Maybe that's what they are supposed to do. My sister would normally have needed oxygen, but they didn't provide it. I felt it was an indication of what was coming. I just kept praying a Psalm out loud and I said to one of her sons, 'Light the candle,' which he did.

She was having great difficulty breathing at this stage and was clinging on to life. One of her sons said, 'This can't go on! It can't go on!' He said it in desperation and I think it helped her to go. Eventually, she passed away. It was around nine or ten o'clock in the evening when she died.

Sometime after my sister's death, my nephew told me what had happened to him back at his house on the night she had died. He told me that when he was resting at home in bed, he distinctly saw his grandfather and his uncle coming towards him. I do not know how he would have recognised his grandfather or his uncle; they had passed away years before. Both of them would have been very fond of the family.

He was awake when it happened. This wasn't a dream; it was for real. He thought they were coming for him and he was frightened. He connected it in that way. He said, 'Please go away!' At that moment, the phone rang and he was told that his mother, my sister, had just died. That was clearly an extraordinary experience.

My nephew was an extremely solid person. He wouldn't exaggerate or hallucinate. He was very down-to-earth and sensible. When he told me, it was obvious that what had occurred had been very real. However, he was very psychic and what happened was uncannily normal to him.

I asked him how he interpreted this visitation. He said, 'Maybe they were thanking me for all the care I had given my mother or maybe they were saying, "It's over now to us, you can rest."' He felt that they had come to him for one of those reasons. They were the only interpretations he could think of.

I accept what happened for what it was. I was in Iona recently and they talk there about a 'thin place'. That thin place is the veil between heaven and earth and it is part of our Celtic heritage. It is a very thin veil indeed. A deceased person can therefore cross back from the other side. I think this is possible. Extraordinary things can happen.

Recently, a small but strange thing occurred involving me. My neighbour had died and a friend of mine who is abroad had known her well. I wrote and told her that this lady had passed away. My friend wrote back and said, 'She has a daughter and I would be grateful if you could get me her address.' I did a bit of research, but I failed to get it.

I said to myself, 'I'll just send an email back and suggest that maybe my friend could write a letter to the mother's address. It might get to the daughter, even though the house is empty.' As I was writing it, I thought, 'Let me just run out and check the address.' I was wondering whether, even though the house was next door, it carried the next street number.

I went out and found the door of the woman's house open. The daughter that I had wanted to contact came out of the house just at that moment. Apparently, she was passing by and had just looked in. Little coincidences like that happen and I wonder about them and about 'thin places'.

I believe deceased relatives come back to those who are dying. I have often heard similar stories and I think they are connected to this thin veil. My brother, for example, said that he saw his mother coming into the room when he was dying, and a lot of people are visited by relatives from the other side. I also believe Jesus can be with the person in their struggle, just like the struggle he went through when he was dying.

I really don't know why it happens. Death, I suppose, is momentous and can be a terrible battle. Maybe the moment of departure can bring peace, but death itself can be an awful wrench for some. As St. Paul says, the last enemy to be put under foot is death. Maybe, then, these things occur to strengthen people who are passing away. Certainly, the type of phenomenon experienced by my nephew does seem to happen and it has happened to many others apart from him.

MARY, FROM COUNTY WATERFORD, details how her dying husband may have witnessed both his deceased son and grandmother shortly before he died.

In May 2007, my husband was diagnosed with cancer. They were giving him a really good chance with chemotherapy. My husband was very upbeat. He never complained or moaned. Unfortunately, around September, I saw a big change coming over him. I could spot it because, two years previously, my father had been through cancer as well. My husband was getting down and very forgetful. He started deteriorating fast.

By October, I had to literally carry him out of the hospital. He wasn't able to drive the car anymore. He was so worn with the chemotherapy. I thought, 'This is not right.' He was then readmitted to hospital. While there, he got sicker and sicker by the day. They eventually got him ready to leave hospital, but he wasn't well when he came home.

He was in and out of hospital right up to Christmas. On

one occasion, he said, 'I was in Aunt Florrie's arms and my grandmother was coming around by the gable-end of the house!' He then asked for a photo of his grandmother. He used to visit her when he was young. He always spoke highly about her. I remembered the photo. He really wanted it and I eventually got him a copy. I gave it to him. He just looked at it and said, 'That's her, that's how I remember her.' I don't know what that was about, but it was strange.

On yet another occasion, he called out our dead son's name, Brendan. Our son had died from meningitis when he was only 20 months old. We had been told, 'He's over the worst, there's no need to send him to hospital.' I asked my husband why he called out Brendan's name, but he wasn't with me or hearing me and he never replied.

On a further occasion, he said, 'You know, I thought I was dead and gone to heaven and if heaven is where I was, I don't mind dying!' I'll never forget those words. He looked very content as he spoke. He was sitting up in the bed at this stage with his arms folded, deep in thought. He seemed a bit confused and puzzled as he said this. I was gobsmacked by what he said, although I didn't speak to him about it. Sadly, we avoided speaking about death, which I now regret.

Then, on Christmas Eve, my husband got worse. He was being fed through a tube at the time. They had so many lines going into him. His breathing was getting very bad. He was yellow in colour. It was all so stressful. I was going to go to Mass on Christmas Eve night, but he was so sick I couldn't leave him.

On Christmas Day, he deteriorated further. I can remember calling a nurse and she came in and said, 'He's going. Talk to him. He'll hear you.' I don't even know what I said to him. The next thing, he opened up his eyes. There was a smile lit up his face. It was like a child's smile. He was so radiant, serene and happy.

He spoke as clear as could be. He said, 'I thought I was in heaven and it was full of flowers!' The nurse looked at me and I looked at her. We were the only two people there. They were the last words he said. He just ebbed away after that. He died at a quarter-to-two on Christmas Day.

All those things will live with me: the radiant smile that lit up his face on Christmas Day, his earlier comment about heaven and how he mentioned his grandmother and our son Brendan. I was astounded by the things that he said. It's not that we were a religious family, although he was really a great Christian.

What he said, especially on Christmas Day, gives me great consolation. When I really get down, I think of his smile. He was so at peace. But, of course, I'm gutted that I haven't him with me. And Christmas Day will never be the same for me again.

SAMMY, FROM COUNTY CORK, recalls what happened when his father passed away in May 1988.

My father, who was also called Sammy, got prostate cancer and he died at 59 years of age. The diagnosis was made in December and he was fine up to about February, but then in March, April and May he went downhill. They discussed treatment, but they said, 'It's not going to work.' The cancer was probably diagnosed too late. He died on 13 May.

It became quite bad near the end. He was in pain and on a lot of medication. They were giving him morphine, but they didn't have the patches like they have today. He also used to get blockages and a retired local doctor, who was brilliant, helped out. We had to feed him and give him water.

We were weeks nursing him. I worked during the day, so I might be with him around the hours of seven o'clock in the evening until one or two o'clock in the morning. Others were there with him, too. The whole family helped out. He had a second wife and she was there along with members of her family. She was great. We would all sit there, talking away.

I always remember him with the Rosary beads. He would lie in the bed, propped up with three pillows behind his back, saying the Rosary. I would sit there and watch the speed of his hands on the beads. Sometimes, the speed would be fast, but then it would slow down. I think the Hail Marys might be faster than the other prayers. It's the funniest things that come back to you. My lasting memories of my father in the bed are of him doing that.

I also remember the smiles that were coming to his face. They started about seven days before he died. He would be saying his Rosary and the next thing he would look up and smile. He'd put his head down again and start on the Rosary beads once more. He would then look up again and smile. This would happen every four or five minutes. The smiles were unusual, especially in the case of a man who was dying and in pain.

It's hard to describe what the smiles were like. All I can see, when I think of them, is sweetness. His lips and two cheeks would come up. It was like he was meeting someone he hadn't met for years. It was as if, on seeing them, he was recognising them and saying, 'Oh, my God!' and a big smile was coming to his face, with the ears popping up and the teeth showing. He looked so happy.

His lips would be moving and it looked like he was talking to those he saw. You would also see his hand moving. It would extend out, as if reaching for someone. He would then smile again and his hand would slowly come back down to the Rosary beads and he would continue on. Whatever it was he was seeing was nice.

Sometimes, he looked from left to right with his eyes. His eyes were really like the windscreen wipers of a car. There might be four of us in the room, one at each side and two others standing at the end of the bed. But it didn't seem like he was looking at us. I was his son and if he saw me you would expect his eyes to stop and focus on me. Maybe he was following somebody. Or maybe a lot of people – his whole family, past and present – were around him. I'd like to think that.

We had a feeling there was a strong presence in the room. All of us felt, 'There's someone with our father.' We asked ourselves, 'Who is it?' We thought our mother, Mena, might be there. She was his first wife and had died years before him, at the age of 51. She had died from lung cancer, caused by smoking. She had a horrible illness, lasting three years. It was very rough.

My father had been so good to her when she was ill. He was unbelievable. There was no better husband and they were very close. We were hoping she was there and was reunited with my father. Others thought it might have been his mother, who had died in 1966. Every one of us had a different opinion about who it was.

We also thought it might have been Padre Pio. My father was a big devotee of his and had serious faith in him. His devotion was huge. At some stage, he did mention that both his wife and Padre Pio were present. One of my sisters told me that this came to light one night while he was reminiscing about when he was young, where he had worked, when he got married and also about his family. He was going back through his life.

My sister said that he would occasionally stop reminiscing

and say, 'Mena is in the corner!' He would then point at the other corner and say, 'The man with the beard is in the other corner!' That was Padre Pio he was referring to. I know that my sister got fairly frightened by it. I wasn't there at the time.

My mother was also a big devotee of Padre Pio and I can remember the morning she died. At half-past-six, she said, 'I can put the chair down now; I have the long road done.' She meant, 'I can rest now.' I prayed to Padre Pio that morning, about half-an-hour before she passed away, asking him to take her. She died half-an-hour later, at eight o'clock.

When my father died, again he passed away half-an-hour after I prayed to Padre Pio to take him. I didn't want him to go through any more than he was already going through. I didn't know whether he was in pain or not, but I felt he was. He couldn't communicate with us and his organs were all starting to shut down. His talking had stopped, although the smiles were still there. My prayers came to pass and my father died peacefully in the end.

Looking back, I believe that my father saw my mother and Padre Pio, if not lots of other relatives and friends, shortly before he passed away. I also believe that he went on to all those people. The possibility that they will also be there for me in the end is something to look forward to.

I wouldn't be an intensely religious person, although I have a little bit of faith in my own way. I don't go to Mass every Sunday, only when I feel like it, but I have my own beliefs. Yet what happened with my father was a very big reassurance. I would hope the same thing will happen to me when I go.

NORA, FROM COUNTY SLIGO, talks about events during a recent death.

There was an incident which I witnessed about a year ago

involving a person who developed renal cancer. The man, who was aged 65, was dying. He only had the disease for nine weeks from diagnosis to the time he passed away. He had deteriorated quickly enough and had lost weight. He also felt very ill near the end.

He was much too far gone for any conventional treatment. Instead, he started a course of medication that didn't involve either chemotherapy or radiotherapy. He opted for the treatment himself, although I'd say the consultant didn't believe it was going to achieve anything. Unfortunately, that's the way it turned out and the treatment didn't work.

I was with him shortly before he died. In all, there were some four family members in the room. He was lying in his hospital bed at the time. He had been in an acute-care ward, but by this stage he had been moved to a single room. It was clear he was going to die.

Probably an hour-and-a-half before he passed away, he suddenly sat up in the bed. Although he was dying, he pushed himself into an upright position. I think people can get a supernatural burst of energy at times like that. He then looked down to the bottom of the bed, at the wall ahead of him. It seemed that he could see somebody he knew.

Suddenly, he said, 'Oh, Jesus, I'm dying!' He then put up his thumb, as if he was acknowledging some person and confirming that everything was OK. He seemed to be acknowledging the person he was seeing in front of him, who was waiting for him. He was a spiritual person and may have believed that Jesus was there, although I wouldn't think it was Jesus or anybody like that. But I don't know who it was; nobody will ever know that.

He stayed sitting up for a short time, maybe two minutes or thereabouts. He sat there with no expression and making no movement, but still looking at the wall opposite him down at the bottom of the bed. He never said anything after that. He just lay back on his pillow, closed his eyes and faded away. He died very peacefully an hour-and-a-half later.

I wasn't surprised by what I had seen. I suppose I knew of those things already, where people have a sense that they are going to die and may have seen somebody. Others who were there wondered who he might have seen. They asked each other about it, but they had no ideas. It could have been family or friends or anybody.

It could have been deceased relatives who had passed on before him. His brother had died young, at the age of 29, from a respiratory arrest. The two of them had been close. His parents had passed away a good number of years ago. His mother had died from cancer and his father from a cardiac arrest. It could have been any of them.

I have seen other examples of this through my nursing profession, mainly with older people as they were dying. There are many things I saw people do. Some might put out their arms in an embrace, as if they were reaching out to somebody they see coming for them. They would put up their two arms in a greeting manner, as if they were about to hold the person in their arms.

Others might sit up, as if they were just greeting somebody. More would have a smile on their face, as if they were seeing a deceased person who meant a lot to them. There might also be a gaze or a stare as they look ahead. They would be the common elements you might see.

I wouldn't have seen these things often, but I certainly would have seen them. They could happen at any time of the day while patients are lying on their beds. They just seem to get a sensation or a feeling that somebody is there. They may not die soon after; it could be days or longer, but they would eventually pass away.

I believe that these things happen and I believe that there is an afterlife. I hope there is one and I often wonder about it. I think it will be a place where you go to and meet other spirits where they all come together.

From what I have seen, I also think people come back to some people but not to everybody. Maybe they come back when the person who is dying was close or maybe they once had a great relationship. I really don't know. But for some people, at least, I believe deceased relatives certainly do come back.

BRIGID, FROM COUNTY LOUTH, describes experiences she had as a nurse and in her personal life.

I clearly remember one woman, in particular, who originally came from Dublin. This was when I was training as a nurse in Manchester in the second half of the 1950s. She was in her early 70s and had already lost her husband. She was quite frail, but I remember she had a bit of a tongue on her. For example, when you would try to help her out of bed she would tell you to go away and leave her alone. She could be abrupt in that respect.

She was in a medical ward, which had 30 beds: 15 on the left and 15 on the right, with lockers in between them. They were all metal beds; there were no fancy beds in those days. They had old steel fireplaces there, about three feet long, and you could light fires which heated the floor through underneath pipes. It was a long ward and she was in the first bed on the left-hand side as you went in. I can still visualise her.

The patients there were generally aged from about 55 up to about 80. Some were mobile; others were not mobile. Most would have heart conditions or cancer or similar problems. Young patients wouldn't be there; they would have been moved on. Although I can't fully recall, I know this woman hadn't had a stroke because she could move her arms and things like that. I think what was wrong with her had to do with her heart. I knew she was dying, although she was still quite lucid.

I remember coming into the ward, one time, along with a colleague, and the woman was chatting away. I went over and asked her if she was alright. Initially, she looked at me, but then she looked behind me. She had a smile on her face. It looked like she was greeting some of her family or someone she knew. There was no fear there.

I turned around because I thought that another nurse had arrived, but nobody had. The nurse who was with me said, 'What's she looking at?' I said, 'I don't know.' The woman then started to speak to her husband. I can't be accurate about his name, but I think it was Tommy. I put my hand on her hand and asked her, 'Are you alright?' She just told me she was speaking to Tommy. She went on speaking to him and she more or less told us to go away.

Her family – I think her daughter and daughter-in-law – came in later on and I told them about the name she had mentioned. They looked at one another and the daughter said, 'That was my daddy. He is dead.' I can't remember how long beforehand he had died, but he was gone.

That sort of thing would happen on a fairly regular basis. It was a common occurrence. The people would always look over my shoulder and they would never be looking directly at me. The deceased would always be behind me. Strangely, it was mostly my left shoulder that those who were dying would stare over, although I don't know why that should be.

The events also seemed to happen mainly at night. I would witness a fair amount of them then. That was probably because at night everybody would be asleep and everything would be very quiet. In contrast, by day there would be a lot of activity going on and you wouldn't notice them as much. By day or night, however, many patients would be talking and the nurses would often think they were just rambling, but afterwards they would realise that there was somebody there.

I wasn't put out by what I saw. When I was younger, I had helped my mum to nurse my maternal grandmother. She was a shopkeeper whose husband had died way before. My mother was only 11 years of age when her father had passed away. When my grandmother was dying, she used to tell my mother to go away and leave her alone. She could be very cross. I would go up and tell her off and then sit down and hold her hand and talk to her.

She talked about how she was witnessing her deceased husband, my grandfather. She was talking to him. I remember I got the fright of my life when she looked over my shoulder. I asked her, 'Granny, who are you talking to?' But she would be away in the past and would continue chatting to him.

Another time, my uncle – my dad's brother – was dying. He was a very holy man and he never married, even though he was once engaged. He came from a farming family and his mother didn't want another woman in the house. He got cancer of the bowel, which can be extremely painful, and he refused morphine. He wanted to suffer and he was in intense pain.

I remember going in to him to hold his hand. He talked to someone, too, although to this day I could not tell you who it was. He looked towards the bottom of the bed and he called out. I remember asking him, 'Are you alright?' He sort of shook himself and looked at me and said, 'Yeah, I'm grand.' He died about an hour later. There definitely was somebody in the room that he could see and I couldn't.

I spoke to priests about all these experiences and many

would say, 'Not at all, you imagined them.' But there was one priest, who had a late vocation, and he was different. I remember he once said, 'The dead do come back. They are always there. They are looking after you.' I suppose that's what I had experienced myself and I had no doubt. I always knew.

I think that those who have passed on come for their own as they are dying. I firmly believe that. No matter what our circumstances are, there are very few of us who have no relations. There's always somebody, be it a grandmother or great-grandmother or whatever, in the background. I really believe they come for you. I have absolutely no doubt from what I have seen. There's nothing that would ever convince me otherwise.

JOHANNA, FROM COUNTY TIPPERARY, recalls events that took place around the death of her father in 2007.

My father was a great person and a decent man. He loved his family and was a Pioneer. Although his hearing was failing, he also loved music. Reading was another of his pastimes. I will always remember him as being up for the underdog. If he saw someone in trouble, he would help them out. A lot of people came to us after he died, telling us their stories. He was a genuinely good man.

Dad had problems with his stomach for years, on and off, but he felt really ill on Christmas Day 2006. He went to the doctor, who didn't make much of it. Then, in January and February, he started to lose weight. We never thought about cancer. I don't know what we were thinking. I suppose we thought, 'It doesn't happen in our family.' We were in denial, I guess.

Around May, he started to feel weak. He took a couple of turns, but he did nothing as I think he believed he had an ulcer. In July, however, he went for an endoscopy and the doctor didn't like anything she saw. She said, 'It's not very good at all.' He was diagnosed as having stomach cancer and he had one dose of chemotherapy. The whole thing was horrendous. There was an infection in the hospital and we weren't allowed in to visit, although eventually we were given permission to enter. My dad was 74 at the time.

One Saturday, in late August, my dad said, 'I want to go home, but I know I can't survive without all this equipment.' He was attached to machines at the time. He could see the machines were keeping him alive. My sister and my mother were with him when he suddenly mentioned the best man from his wedding and said he had come to visit. He was smiling at the time. He said, 'Christy has come to see me!' which was strange because Christy had died in 1999. When I heard about what he said, I thought, 'Christy is going to look after my dad from here on in.' I think my dad felt safe after what he saw.

On the following day, the Sunday, I went in to see him. He was in a little ward of his own and was lying back in the bed. He was on drips and he was drifting into another world. His eyes were really blue and open. He was very thin and weak. That day, he went through his family history and talked about things he'd like to do. He reminisced a lot. But I felt he was looking into a different place. He had a sort of gaze on his face as he was looking at something that obviously we couldn't see.

All of that day, I thought he was in communion with something or with somebody else. I really felt his best man was looking after him. I also thought his brother was taking care of him. He had previously said, one night while he was still at home, 'I heard Michael out in the kitchen!' Michael was his older brother, my uncle, who had died back in 1994. He really thought he had heard Michael there. So I feel that my uncle was assisting him as well.

My father died on Sunday, 26 August 2007. He had had enough of the illness, the treatment and the whole horrible scenario. Although he never wanted to die, he asked God to take him in the end. I wasn't happy that he was leaving us, but I felt he was going somewhere better and Christy and Michael were going to look after him. It was a lovely feeling.

It wasn't the only experience like this that I came across. My father-in-law also had something similar happen to him around the time of his death. He had lost his daughter tragically when she was very young. She was an absolutely beautiful girl. When he was dying, he said he had seen her and she looked the same as ever. He asked the others, 'Can't you see her?' Although no one else could, he could. I really believe that she came to take him home.

I love to believe that all these things indicate that there is something more after we die. Not every person would agree. People make remarks like, 'When you're dead, you're dead.' They also say, 'Well, the dead never come back to tell us.' You have all different types of mindset.

I think there are things that those who have passed away cannot do. There are also things they can do. For example, I believe that when we need comfort they can give us a sign. And I believe they come to us at the time of our death. From what I've found out myself, I'm sure they do.

TOM, FROM COUNTY CORK, describes a colourful deathbed vision involving his grandmother, Kilkenny woman Catherine Doyle.

My grandmother died in January 2003. We reckon she was over 100 years of age when she passed away, but we actually didn't know what her genuine age was. During the War of

Independence, a number of her records had been destroyed. However, from the time I was a little fellow, she would always say that she was only 39 years old.

She had stolen that line about being 39 from the legendary American comedian Jack Benny. He used to always say that. As a result, whenever I'd ask her how old she was, she would say, 'I'm only 39.' Because of that, when she died they put her age as 93 on her grave; they just reversed the 39.

The two of us were very close. I was mad about her. She was a wonderful woman, but had a tough life. As a young girl, she was sold into a thing called 'bonded servitude'. She also never learned how to read or write. Her husband, my grandfather, had died young. Towards the end of her life, she had to be looked after by my aunt and uncle. She was very frail and was bedridden for probably 20 years.

I would visit her a lot up in Kilkenny. She used to call me 'John Wayne', after the cowboy actor. That was her nickname for me. I would just call her 'Kate'. I would go into her bedroom and she'd say. 'I haven't seen you for ages, John Wayne. Go on! Hop it! Get out of here!' I would say, in a cowboy accent, 'Well, hell there, Kate Doyle!' She'd say, 'You're nothing but an impudent brat.' She'd then put a smirk on her face and say, 'I'm so glad to see you.'

One day, two or three weeks before she died, I went to visit her. On my way in, I asked my aunt, 'How's herself?' She said, 'You're not going to believe me, but she looks as if she's wearing make-up in the bed. Go down and see her.' I went down and she did look different. Her lips were red and she looked like she had rouge on her cheeks. There was a sparkle in her eyes. I felt her face, but it wasn't make-up. It was just that she looked so well. She just looked as if she was made-up.

I said, 'Well, Kate, are you getting ready to go dancing?'

She said, 'I'm not, but I won't be with you long. The angels came to me during the night. They took me to a place and showed me where I'm going to be going. I saw colours there that I never saw before. There were animals there that I never saw before either. The most beautiful flowers were there; some of them were singing and some of them playing music, and all to the glory of God!'

She told me it all in such perfect detail. She was totally lucid. I said, 'Kate, whatever you were on, give me some of it, I'd love to have it.' But she said, 'Go away, you impudent brat. I'm telling you the truth and you can believe me if you like.' We then started talking about everyday things and I suppose I really just dismissed what she said as a bit of a joke.

I later told my aunt, who was elsewhere in the house, and she got upset. She said, 'I want to tell you something. When I was with her, a day ago, she pulled the bedclothes back. She said, "Come here, daughter, I want you to lie down alongside me." She then put the bedclothes over me and said, "Thanks for looking after me, but I'm going to look after you very soon for the rest of your life."' My aunt then said, 'Tom, I don't know what's going to happen.' I said, 'Don't worry. She's only doting.'

About a fortnight later, I was walking down the street in a town in County Cork. I was thinking about my grandmother and saying that on the coming weekend I was going to bring my young granddaughter up to see her. They had never met, although my grandmother had seen photos of her. But, at around 12 o'clock, I got a phone call telling me that my grandmother had passed away.

I thought no more about it until some years later when I was sitting at home and looking at one of the satellite channels on TV. A little girl was on, telling her story about how she had died on the operating table in hospital. What she said was the exact same thing that my grandmother told me. She said she was taken to a beautiful place, with colours she had never seen before. There were animals there that she had never seen before either. The flowers were beautiful, with some of them singing songs and others playing music.

I was glued to the box. I didn't know what to think. I said, 'How can this be?' I found it all so extraordinary. Here I was, years down the road, watching a girl from America telling exactly the same story that my grandmother told me two or three weeks before she died. They didn't know each other or even know that each other had existed, yet they described the very same thing.

It wasn't as if my grandmother was very religious. She wasn't a Mass goer, even before she became bedridden. Nor am I very religious either. I don't go to Mass regularly or to the sacraments regularly. I just go when I feel like going. But I think what they were both describing was an ethereal heaven, a place beyond here, somewhere extraordinary, a place that cannot be explained.

Although I am not very religious, I have always had a great belief in God. I believe that the living rock cannot exist without it knowing God and without God knowing it. So I definitely believe there's another dimension. And I believe that my grandmother got a glimpse of it that time, back in 2003, shortly before she died.

VINNY, FROM COUNTY GALWAY, recalls his uncle's deathbed vision. It consisted of the appearance of hands, as if a figure had arrived, and images of water. Vinny believes that what took place was a visit from Christ.

My uncle was diagnosed with bone marrow cancer after he had just turned 50. He was a farmer and a very simple man.

Married with a couple of kids, he appreciated his bacon and cabbage on a Sunday. He was also hugely respected and was a great singer. I suppose that you would call him a typical Irish country farmer and a man of the land.

He was diagnosed in springtime and he declined rapidly. I had always noticed that he was such a strong man, both physically and mentally, but he deteriorated very quickly. He faded fast. The cancer was rapid and fierce. He ended up on morphine, but it didn't seem to kill the pain and the chemotherapy didn't kill the disease. It just ravaged through him.

Around the middle of September, it was clear that he was dying. He was at home at this stage and pretty much in a coma. He wasn't communicating in any shape or form. He was in his bedroom, lying on the left-hand side of the double bed. His sisters – my mother and aunt – were beside the bed. They were very basic people and believed in prayer. They were praying away. I was elsewhere in the house at the time.

At 3 pm, he suddenly shot up in the bed and he was very alert. His eyes were wide open and he was totally conscious. His sisters were in the middle of the Divine Mercy at the time. He said, 'All around me, I can see water!' He thought there was a leak in the roof. It was strange because he had grown up near water, but he couldn't fathom what the water he saw was about. My mother said later that it was strange that for a man so familiar with water he seemed to be seeing more water than he ever saw in his life.

He then said, 'God! Look at the hands!' His hands were out in front of him as he said this. He had stretched them out with the palms facing up, exactly like they are in the Divine Mercy picture. It was like he was mimicking what he saw. Someone said, 'There are no hands. We can't see any hands.' But he was very sharp and said, 'They are there. I can see them. And I can see all the water. Look at all the water, it is endless!'

He stayed looking for a while and then he fell back on the bed. He went back into a sort of coma. His sisters continued praying, with their heads down. He died nine hours later, just following midnight. I was with him at the time. It was a merciful release because he had suffered so long. He had really endured enough, God love him.

It was only after he was buried that my aunt and mother thought about what had happened. It was only then that the penny dropped about what was going on. They looked at the prayers of the Divine Mercy and saw Christ say that he will come. They believed that it was Christ had come to meet him. They blessed themselves and said, 'Thank God for that!'

I also have faith in the Divine Mercy. In it, Christ says, 'Whoever will recite it will receive great mercy at the hour of death.' One of the prayers refers to 'the ocean of mercy.' From my perspective, I felt that the water my uncle saw was 'the ocean of mercy.' Another one of the prayers is that Christ will come as a merciful saviour, not as judge. I believe that what he did was he came as a merciful saviour. He was coming for my uncle from heaven.

What happened gave great comfort to those around him, especially to his sisters. It was a lovely experience for us left behind to believe that God had shown him this. We felt that Christ was near him. It was also lovely to see the fulfilling of the promises in the Divine Mercy. I think what happened gave him hope in the midst of his sickness. And I really believe it was God or something divine had come to help guide him across.

CHRISTY, WHO COMES FROM COUNTY TIPPERARY but who lives in the UK, outlines what took place when his wife passed away in 2008.

My wife, Nora, and I both came from County Tipperary, but we moved to the UK. We had lived a mile-and-a-half from each other at home. We met in Ireland, but she then moved over to England. I came after her in October 1957. I worked with the Ford Motor Company for 27 years. Nora was an auxiliary nurse for a while.

We got married in Dagenham in 1959 and we had six children: three boys and three girls. With a family of that size, there was no time for her to work, so she looked after the children. I worked on in Ford's. Eventually, after 27 years, I was made redundant and went gardening. I was happy with that and did it for the rest of my working life.

Nora was a lovely woman. We had a wonderful life. We remained 'Irish'. My accent never changed and nor did Nora's. People used to say it was harder to understand her than me. We used to go home to Tipperary every couple of years. We used to take the kids in my old Corsair car. We kept on doing that until they became too big and developed lives of their own.

Eventually, in late 2007, my wife developed cancer. The doctor was treating her for a prolapsed womb. However, we went in one day to see a gynaecologist and he said, 'You have a tumour.' That was the start of it. Her cancer eventually spread all around her stomach. It was very bad news and there was no cure.

She had to be hospitalised. She was only in for 11 days. Things went wrong while she was there. She fell at one stage. She had gone out to the toilet. She came back into bed, but was only there a few minutes when she decided to get out again. She collapsed on the floor. I think she was confused and didn't know where she was. That was a setback.

She faded quickly. In the last three days, she didn't really know we were there. I remember once saying, 'If you know who's talking to you, give my hand a squeeze.' But she never did. She never spoke to any of us. She only spoke once and that was when an old friend came in, who was Italian. The lady said, 'Hello, Nora.' She replied, 'Hello, Lucie.' That was the only thing she said to anyone in conversation in those three days.

She did, however, say something else. I was alone with her at the time. She repeated on three occasions, 'Where's Mary and Breda?' I knew who Mary must have been. She was her sister, who had died six months before. She had lived in Tipperary. She was about a year-and-a-half older. They had been close.

I had no idea who Breda was. It was only on Nora's last day alive that her sister, Anna, came over from Ireland. I asked her, 'Can you tell me who Breda is? She is trying to find her.' She told me that Breda was her sister, who had died in a fire when she was very young. She was only something like 12 or 18 months old.

What happened was that my wife's mother used to do the First Fridays. She left her father, who was Nora's grand-father, to look after Breda. There was no one else in the house apart from the two of them. At one stage, he walked about 100 yards to the well to get some water. It was only over the road. When he came back, he couldn't find Breda.

He eventually found her down under the bed. What had happened was that he had left a pot on the fire with a lid on it so that she wouldn't go near it. It seems she must have shifted the lid. Her nightdress caught fire. But she didn't die from burns; she just crawled under the bed and died from fright.

Nora said 'Where's Mary and Breda?' three times to me. I don't know if she said it to anyone else. She was trying to find them. I got the impression, and seem to recall, that she found Mary. Mary had seemingly come to her. I think she might have said something about that to me. It was all so strange to me at the time and I didn't take it all in. But she couldn't find Breda and it was really her that she was trying to find.

My wife passed away on 27 February 2008, after 49 years of marriage. She had lasted only 11 days in hospital. And I don't know if she ever found Breda. We buried her in County Tipperary and I go over every year for her anniversary.

I eventually described to a friend of mine what she had said in the hospital. He told me he had been very sick years ago and had to be escorted to the hospital by the police. He said he had died twice in the ambulance. He said he had met his deceased dad and mum in a tunnel. They were there to greet him. They told him, 'You shouldn't be here! You can go back!' He came back and survived.

I think the whole thing that happened with Nora puzzled me mainly because I didn't know about Breda, although I knew Mary very well. Yet I wasn't really surprised that it happened. I believe these things occur and, in the same way, I will more than likely meet my wife again. I think she will be waiting for me and will come to greet me. I'd expect to meet everyone that I know who passed away. I don't think about it too much and I don't dwell on it. I just expect it to happen and I think it will.

Margaret, from County Longford, tells how a young neighbour received a visit from his deceased mother shortly before he died.

There was a young man who lived down the road from me. He was a lovely person, a really nice human being. He would help people with the hay and work really hard. He didn't recognise the extent of his strength and I would say to him, 'Take it easy. Be easy on yourself.' He was nice to everybody.

To give you an example of how kind he was, he used to go to town on the odd night and he would just have one pint. He would then walk home. Because our house was so close to the road, and my husband sometimes worked nights, he thought that if I heard steps on the road I might be afraid. So he would start to sing as he walked along to make sure that I knew it was him. That will show you how considerate he was.

There were a lot of children in his family and their mother had died from a heart attack when they were young. As a result, I used to help them with their homework and give them their dinners when they would be coming home from school. Their father used to say that I had partially adopted them. This young man, however, was a little bit slow and was sent to a special school. He would also come in to visit me and we would both chat away. He loved his bread and strawberry jam.

When he was just going on 21, he came in to me one morning and he was sitting in the kitchen. He said, 'I saw Mammy last night!' His mother had been dead for four or five years at this stage. I said, 'Did you have a lot to drink last night?' 'No,' he said, 'I always only drink one pint. You know that.'

I asked him, 'Where did you see your mother? Was it

in a dream?' 'No,' he said, 'I was just walking home.' As it happened, there were two routes he could take to walk home and he didn't take the one past our house; he took the other one. 'I was at the bridge, coming across the other road,' he said. I then asked him, 'Was it dark?' 'It was,' he said, 'and I was walking along, singing to myself, when Mammy came to me.'

'Was it in your head that she came to you,' I wondered, 'or did you see her physically?' He said, 'I could see her face in the dark.' 'Were you afraid?' I also wondered. 'No,' he said, 'it was Mammy.' So I asked him if she had said anything and he said, 'Yeah. She said, "I'm coming for you soon!"'

To reassure him, I said, 'That's interesting, but you have to realise that when people go to God, time is different for them than it is for us. "Soon" for your mother could be the same as 50 years for you. That might be quick for her because she is in such a wonderful place. What she was talking about might be a long way off.' I didn't know what to say or think because I was so concerned for him. I suggested that he didn't mention what had happened to anybody else. I said, 'Why don't we keep it between ourselves?'

Within a week, his twenty-first birthday was coming up. The special school he was in were taking them on a tour to the Phoenix Park, in Dublin, to visit the Zoo and places like that. The night beforehand, he was talking to me and he was all excited. He hadn't been to the Zoo and was thrilled at the thought. So off they went up to Dublin. Unfortunately, he dropped dead in the Phoenix Park.

I was absolutely stunned when I heard the news. It wasn't anticipated. It was totally out of the blue. His father was called and told the news. He sent someone down to my house to tell me what had happened. I think the first thing I said was, 'My God! His mother really was coming for him. And she came soon.' That was the very first thing I thought of, probably because it was less than a week since he had told me what he had seen. It was fresh in my head.

I have never forgotten what happened and I think about it now and then. I have been through tough times in my own life. I've had heart attacks, a stroke and cancer. I've been unconscious and in Intensive Care. There was big talk that I was going to die. Although my life hasn't been easy, God has never left me.

I strongly believe in God. He has been with me through every bit of it. And I'm flying. I feel so much better now. We might not always be aware of all the help we are getting, but I believe that I am being helped through. And I believe that in my case and in the case of that young man, God is good.

Looking back, I think that in certain cases God allows those who have passed on to help us. I believe this young man's mother was taking care of him. I think she was telling him, 'Everything is fine! I am here and coming for you!' She knew he was going to die.

After they checked his medical history and that of his family, they found out that he had a heart problem and that the reason he was slow was that oxygen wasn't getting to his brain quickly enough. They found the same condition in his brother, who died within 12 months, at the age of 23. She knew what was coming.

It was interesting that she didn't scare him. I think that's why I believe in it. He wasn't afraid when I asked him if he was frightened. He said, 'No, it was Mammy.' He wasn't worried at all. He wasn't panicking or wondering, 'My God! I'm going to die!' That never bothered him because he was reassured by his mother. He knew it was his mother and that she was caring for him. He knew she was coming.

JOSEPHINE, FROM COUNTY WATERFORD, worked as a nurse in a hospital where she witnessed many deathbed visions.

I remember one old man, back around 35 years ago. He was in very severe pain, with cancer of the bones. His cancer had started elsewhere, but by the time he came to us it had spread to the bones and there wasn't any hope. He was crying out and I'd say he was suffering a lot. Pain relief wasn't as good in those days. Nowadays, patients have their own morphine-pumps and are allowed to use them when they need them, but that wasn't done at that time.

He had been with us for three or four weeks. Towards the end, he was just a shadow of himself, in a very bad way. I remember he was screened off in the corner of the ward. The hospital did have a number of private rooms, but there wasn't one vacant. That wasn't good for the other patients, listening to what was going on. It wasn't good for him either, and I'm sure his friends must have been shocked at how bad he looked.

I got to know him well. Initially, I had nursed him on days and then, by the time my night duty came around, I knew a lot about him. I knew, in particular, that he was coming to an end and that he was going to die. Two nurses were on nights and we knew that one of us would have to stay with him. I was the one with him on the night he died. He was in a bad way at the time, with laboured breathing and you could hear the death-rattle.

Suddenly, he sat up in the bed, with his arms out, calling, 'Mammy!' It was as if he had seen something wonderful. The way he did it, and the way he leaned forward, it was like as if his mother was at the end of the bed. All the pain left him and you could see the peace setting in. Everything eased and his face relaxed. His smile was remarkable. A peaceful look came over him. He then eased back on the pillow and he was gone.

It was strange to see an old man do this. He was well into his 70s and it was very odd to hear him saying, 'Mammy!' I mean, most people don't have a mammy at that stage. Yet it really had to be his mother that he was seeing. And it had a big impact on him. You can imagine what his face had looked like because of the pain. You couldn't believe the change or that he was the same man.

Another time, I was nursing an old lady who was dying from old age. Her family were in and out all the time. One night, she was low and her family stayed late. Eventually, she seemed to get comfortable, so they went home saying, 'We'll be back in the morning.'

At about two o'clock in the morning, we were checking on the woman and making her comfortable. She was awake again at this stage. She said, 'Don't go. Don't leave me. I don't want to be on my own.' The woman was afraid of dying. Although she was worried, it didn't seem that she was about to die.

The next thing, she got a look of peace on her face. It was a vacant, faraway look. She looked dazed, staring into the distance, as if she wasn't seeing us at all. She had been so low beforehand, as if she was going to go unconscious, but suddenly she was beaming. You could see she was experiencing something wonderful. She then looked at us. 'Oh! Johnny! Johnny is here!' she said. She said it so clearly. She died practically as she was saying it. We immediately wondered who Johnny was. We had no idea.

The next day, we had to inform the relatives and I was talking to the woman's son. I asked him, 'Would you tell me who Johnny is?' 'How did you know?' he said. Straight away, he explained, 'That was my father, who is dead.' So I told him what she had said and explained that we hadn't known it was her husband. 'She must have seen him and he must have come to meet her,' he replied. I think he was really thrilled that his father had come to his mother.

On a further occasion, I was nursing a young child, aged five, who was dying. He had leukaemia and they couldn't treat him. He had been in and out of hospital and was in a very bad way. He was on the children's ward, where I was working at the time. His parents were in and out and didn't expect him to survive long. One particular night, we said, 'He may die tonight. Someone needs to be with him.' I was the one chosen.

When I was with him, suddenly he opened up his eyes and started smiling. He was looking into the far distance, like he was in a sort of a trance. Everything went very peaceful, very quiet, and he looked like a little angel. Suddenly, he started calling for his nana.

His mother was there at the time. She was looking at me and I was looking at her. His mother then told me that his grandmother had died about a month beforehand. It was all very strange. Even though his parents were there, it was his nana he was calling, although she was dead. Obviously, he must have seen her. He died soon after that.

There are many similar stories, although they may not be as common today. I think there are many reasons for that. For a start, people die much less at home, where a lot of other people would be in contact with them. At one time, people died in their bedrooms or in a general hospital ward, around other people; they are now more likely to be moved to a hospice. As a result, people don't see these things happening like they used to.

Another factor is the short-staffing in hospitals. Nurses don't have time to spend with patients anymore. It is a terrible pity. When you are admitted to hospital, you are just like a number. There is no proper contact between staff and patients. That's the view of a lot of nurses and it means that they don't see much of what's going on in their patients' personal lives. It is a definite factor.

Also, people who are dying can differ. A lot of them just quietly drift off and you don't see anything. You might go in to check on them and find they have quietly passed away. You take their pulse and discover that they are dead. Other times, you might see people who just drift off as if they are falling asleep. You would notice nothing in those cases. It doesn't, of course, mean that nothing has happened.

Furthermore, like life, there are so many different types of people. Some people would love to tell you about things; others are private and won't tell you anything. You come across the latter a lot. Again, some people are happier to be on their own; others might be scared and want somebody with them. It's only when you are with them that you'd become aware of what's going on.

People also cope differently. For example, I once nursed a young woman in her early 50s who was dying of pancreatic cancer. She was a lovely woman and I got to know her quite well. I remember coming on duty one May morning and it was a beautiful day. The sun was shining in the windows. The other nurse who was on with me said, 'Would you ever go in and look after her. She had a bad night and I don't think she will last much longer.'

I dropped my coat and bag and went in to her to say hello. The moment I went in, she said, 'I'm so glad you are here.' I said, 'How are you? I hear you didn't have a good night.' 'I've just been hanging on,' she said. 'Will you fix the pillow for me?' So I fixed the pillow and eased her back. She then asked me to hold her hand. I held her two hands and she said, 'I'm ready to go now.' And she died. She was obviously waiting. Maybe other people wait for dead relatives to arrive instead.

Having come across so many real-life examples of these experiences and seen people's reactions, I think there must be something better after we die. You must remember that the people who come to the dying have passed on. If they just disappeared completely and there was nowhere else to go to, their relatives who are dying wouldn't see them again. If someone is seeing a husband or mother who is dead for years, they wouldn't see them again if death was the end. It makes me feel there must be something there.

What happens is also very real. You can see the change in people, especially in those who are ravaged by pain. Their countenance is transformed. It obviously makes them feel good. It helps their families as well. It makes you feel good, too, especially after you have been helping them through hard times. You feel, 'They have been through hell, but there's definitely a reward there.'

Ultimately, I suppose, we are all sceptical. I am, too. I wouldn't believe in everything I see. I would wonder about things. And there are things I don't believe in. But I definitely think there is something to this. A lot of nurses who are dealing with the dying come across many examples and they talk about them between themselves. They happen a lot. And I think if you are there and you experience one, you would say, 'There is definitely something out there.'

D.P. Kidder was the first modern-day, non-fiction chronicler of deathbed visions. The stories he compiled were published in 1848 in his book *The Dying Hours of Good and Bad Men Contrasted*. This brief extract, which features the appearance of a dying man's deceased wife and angelic

spirits, illustrates how deathbed vision reports have remained largely consistent throughout the ages.

The Rev. Enoch George died in Staunton, Virginia, August 23, 1828. In early life he became pious, and, under a strong conviction that it was his duty to preach the gospel, entered the travelling ministry of the Methodist Episcopal Church. His success gave the fullest demonstration that he was not mistaken in his calling. In 1816 he was elected bishop in said church, in which office he continued until his death. His piety was deep, and was strikingly exemplified in life and in death.

His end was remarkably peaceful. To several brethren, who called to see him a short time before his death, he said, 'If I die, I am going to glory! For this I have been living forty years.' He made arrangements for the settlement of his temporal affairs with much composure. He requested that the fourteenth and fifteenth chapters of the Gospel by St. John might be read. On hearing them, he made some appropriate remarks on the sentiments contained in them, and exclaimed, 'What a body of divinity and valuable truth is contained in those chapters?' His soul was filled with great joy.

On one occasion he said to a friend, who expressed a desire for him to live longer, 'Why do you not wish me to go to heaven from Staunton?' His sufferings at times were great, but he bore them patiently. 'Glory! Glory!' was his theme. To his attendant physician he said, 'I shall soon be in glory!'

In the ecstasy of his feelings he appears to have been greatly abstracted from the world, and absorbed in meditations on the enjoyment of the society of glorified spirits – so much so as to have lost himself in the raptures of the glory just ready to break upon him, if he were not already favoured with a vision of angelic attendants.

He said to a friend, 'Who are these? Are they not all ministering spirits? My dear departed wife has been with me, and I shall soon be with her in glory.' As several brethren entered the room to see him, he raised his arms to embrace them, and said, 'Brethren, rejoice with me; I am going to glory.' As his strength failed, his joys increased. He clapped his hands and exclaimed, 'Shout glory to God!' At another time he said, 'I have been many years trying to lead others to glory, and now thither I am going. For me to live is Christ, but to die is gain.' Thus he expired.

The following three case histories have been extracted from *The Peak in Darien*, which was written by Frances Power Cobbe and published in 1882, more than three decades after D. P. Kidder published his seminal work. The stories were related to Cobbe by a reliable friend.

I was watching one night beside a poor man dying of consumption. His case was hopeless, but there was no appearance of the end being very near. He was in full possession of his senses, able to talk with a strong voice, and not in the least drowsy. He had slept through the day, and was so wakeful that I had been conversing with him on ordinary subjects to while away the long hours.

Suddenly, while we were thus talking quietly together, he became silent, and fixed his eyes on one particular spot in the room, which was entirely vacant, even of furniture. At the same time, a look of the greatest delight changed the whole expression of his face, and, after a moment of what seemed to be intense scrutiny of some object invisible to me, he said to me in a joyous tone, 'There is Jim.'

Jim was a little son whom he had lost the year before, and whom I had known well; but the dying man had a son still living, named John, for whom we had sent, and I concluded it was of John he was speaking, and that he thought he heard him arriving. So I answered, 'No. John has not been able to come.' The man turned to me impatiently, and said: 'I do not mean John, I know he is not here: it is Jim, my little lame Jim. Surely, you remember him?'

'Yes,' I said, 'I remember dear little Jim who died last year quite well.' 'Don't you see him, then? There he is,' said the man, pointing to the vacant space on which his eyes were fixed; and, when I did not answer, he repeated almost fretfully, 'Don't you see him standing there?'

I answered that I could not see him, though I felt perfectly convinced that something was visible to the sick man, which I could not perceive. When I gave him this answer, he seemed quite amazed, and turned round to look at me with a glance almost of indignation. As his eyes met mine, I saw that a film seemed to pass over them, the light of intelligence died away, he gave a gentle sigh and expired. He did not live five minutes from the time he first said, 'There is Jim,' although there had been no sign of approaching death previous to that moment.

The second case was that of a boy about fourteen years of age, dying also of decline. He was a refined, highly educated child, who throughout his long illness had looked forward with much hope and longing to the unknown life to which he believed he was hastening. On a bright summer morning, it became evident that he had reached his last hour. He lost the power of speech, chiefly from weakness; but he was perfectly sensible, and made his wishes known to us by his intelligent looks.

He was sitting propped up in bed, and had been looking rather sadly at the bright sunshine playing on the trees outside his open window for some time. He had turned away from this scene, however, and was facing the end of the room, where there was nothing whatever but a closed

103

door, when all in a moment the whole expression of his face changed to one of the most wondering rapture, which made his half-closed eyes open to their utmost extent, while his lips parted with a smile of perfect ecstasy.

It was impossible to doubt that some glorious sight was visible to him; and, from the movement of his eyes, it was plain that it was not one, but many objects on which he gazed, for his look passed slowly from end to end of what seemed to be the vacant wall before him, going back and forward with ever-increasing delight manifested in his whole aspect.

His mother then asked him, if what he saw was some wonderful sight beyond the confines of this world, to give her a token that it was so by pressing her hand. He at once took her hand, and pressed it meaningly, giving thereby an intelligent affirmative to her question, though unable to speak. As he did so, a change passed over his face, his eyes closed, and in a few minutes he was gone.

The third case, which was that of my own brother, was very similar to this last. He was an elderly man, dying of a painful disease, but one which never for a moment obscured his faculties. Although it was known to be incurable, he had been told that he might live some months, when somewhat suddenly the summons came on a dark January morning. It had been seen in the course of the night that he was sinking; but for some time he had been perfectly silent and motionless, apparently in a state of stupor, his eyes closed and his breathing scarcely perceptible.

As the tardy dawn of the winter morning revealed the rigid features of the countenance from which life and intelligence seemed to have quite departed, those who watched him felt uncertain whether he still lived; but suddenly, while they bent over him to ascertain the truth, he opened his eyes wide, and gazed eagerly upward with such an unmistakable expression of wonder and joy that a thrill of awe passed through all who witnessed it.

His whole face grew bright with a strange gladness, while the eloquent eyes seemed literally to shine, as if reflecting some light on which they gazed. He remained in this attitude of delighted surprise for some minutes, then in a moment the eyelids fell, the head drooped forward, and with one long breath the spirit departed.

Back in 1908, some 26 years following Frances Power Cobbe's *The Peak in Darien*, the well-known researcher Dr. James H. Hyslop, in his esteemed book *Psychical Research and the Resurrection*, chronicled many additional case histories of deathbed visions. The following brief account was provided to him by a Dr. Wilson, who witnessed the death of tenor James Moore.

It was about four o'clock, and the dawn for which he had been watching was creeping in through the shutters, when, as I bent over the bed, I noticed that his face was quite calm and his eyes clear. The poor fellow looked up into my face, and, taking my hand in both of his, he said: 'You've been a good friend to me, doctor. You've stood by me.'

Then something which I shall never forget to my dying day happened; something which is utterly indescribable. While he appeared perfectly rational and as sane as any man I have ever seen, the only way that I can express it is that he was transported into another world and although I cannot satisfactorily explain the matter to myself, I am fully convinced that he had entered the Golden City – for he said in a stronger voice than he had used since I had attended him: 'There is mother! Why, mother, have you come here to see me? No, no, I'm coming to see *you*. Just wait, mother, I am almost over. I can jump it. Wait, mother.'

On his face there was a look of inexpressible happiness, and the way in which he said the words impressed me as I have never been before, and I am as firmly convinced that he saw and talked with his mother as I am that I am sitting here.

In order to preserve what I believed to be his conversation with his mother, and also to have a record of the strangest happening of my life, I immediately wrote down every word he had said. His was one of the most beautiful deaths I have ever seen.

A further 18 years on, in 1926, Sir William Barrett's *Death-Bed Visions* **was released to public astonishment. The book included many case histories, among them the following brief examples provided by a nurse who worked in a large hospital. Once again, they show how deathbed vision narratives have changed little over time.**

I recall the death of a woman (Mrs. Brown, aged 36) who was the victim of that most dreadful disease, malignant cancer. Her sufferings were excruciating, and she prayed earnestly that death might speedily come to her and end her agony.

Suddenly her sufferings appeared to cease; the expression of her face, which a moment before had been distorted by pain, changed to one of radiant joy. Gazing upwards, with a glad light in her eyes, she raised her hands and exclaimed, 'Oh, mother dear, you have come to take me home. I am so glad!' And in another moment her physical life had ceased.

The memory of another death which occurred about the same time comes back to me. It was that of an old soldier who was in the last stages of tuberculosis brought on by exposure while fighting his country's battles. He was brave and patient but had frequent paroxysms of pain that were almost unendurable, and he longed for the relief which he knew death alone could bring him.

One of these spasms had seized upon him, and his features were convulsed with agony as he fought for breath, when he suddenly grew calm. A smile lit up his face, and looking upwards he exclaimed, with a ring of joy in his voice, 'Marion, my daughter!' Then the end came.

His brother and sister were at the bedside. The sister said to the brother, 'He saw Marion, his favourite daughter. She came and took him where he will suffer no more.' And she added fervently, 'Thank God! He has found rest at last.'

NEAR-DEATH
ENCOUNTERS

Almost 2,500 years ago, the Greek philosopher Plato put on record an extraordinary account of a near-death experience. It was the first detailed recording of the phenomenon. The person whose story he chronicled in his book *The Republic* was a warrior soldier by the name of Er, whose slain body was found on the battlefield. Unaffected by decay, it was brought home for burial.

Twelve days after his death, while lying on his funeral pyre, Er came back to life and recalled details of a journey to the other side. What he described has remarkable resonance today. Not only does it replicate in close detail modern-day versions of what we currently refer to as the near-death experience, but it also gives us an understanding of how the phenomenon was perceived hundreds of years before Christ. In addition, he described meetings with deceased souls.

Er explained how shortly after his 'soul left the body,' he and his companions departed on a journey to a 'mysterious place.' There, they encountered newly-dead people ascending out of the earth 'dusty and worn with travel.' They also came across souls descending out of heaven 'clean and bright.' All seemed to have undertaken lengthy journeys.

In an extraordinary evocation of modern-day accounts, Er depicted delightful reunions. 'Those who knew one another embraced and conversed,' he reported, 'the souls which came from earth curiously enquiring about the things above, and the souls which came from heaven about the things beneath.' Those from above described 'heavenly delights and visions of inconceivable beauty.'

Er also referred to 'the light,' which is undoubtedly the one feature of the near-death experience that is most commonly alluded to in modern times. He described it as 'a line of light, straight as a column ... in colour resembling the rainbow, only brighter and purer.' The light he depicted as being 'the belt of heaven' holding together the universe.

He additionally acquainted us with the judgement of souls and his eventual return to real life. Using the familiar language of modern-day accounts, Plato informed us regarding Er, 'In what manner or by what means he returned to the body he could not say.' It's a commonly-used phrase to this day.

This astonishing journey, which was chronicled by Plato sometime around 380 BC, was eventually complemented by a multitude of accounts from early, medieval, Victorian and modern times. All these narratives described extraordinarily similar meetings between the newly-dead or dying and those who were long gone.

What follows updates these many accounts with the latest, previously-unpublished, Irish near-death experiences related to me following the publication of my books *Going Home* and *The Distant Shore*. All are authoritative near-death journeys. More importantly, all of them contain meetings with deceased relatives or friends or, in one case, a possible encounter with a religious figure. The details in all cases are similar to what happens during deathbed visions.

CHRISTY, FROM COUNTY CLARE, met his deceased brother Paul while undergoing a near-death experience following an accident.

I was working as a plumber back in 1990. One Friday, I was

asked to fix a leak on the road. Normally, on a Friday, if you had a problem that could be carried over, you wouldn't get too involved in it. The reason is that it could turn out to be a bigger problem and extend into the weekend. If it looked like a minor job, or if it was a real emergency, you would do it. In this case, we decided to fix it, hoping it wouldn't take too long.

The hole that was made was extremely small and it was full of water. I was wearing waders. I went down into the hole, intending to cut out the broken piece of pipe and put a new piece in. I had the pipe propped up with my toe and I was cutting with a hacksaw. I was cutting through the pipe when, the next thing, everything was electrically live.

I got such a bang! I got blown out of the hole. The force of it was like being hit by two buses. It seemed that there was a big leakage of electricity from somewhere, although I had never heard of this happening before. I really don't know what it was. Either way, I took the whole of the impact. I remember saying, 'I can't take this!' I felt I was gone.

The next thing, I was out of my body, floating away. I felt like a leaf blown away by the wind. I was probably about 30 feet up, getting a bird's-eye view. I could actually see myself on the ground, lying there on my back and looking up. There was no life in me and I couldn't feel any pain. I felt the real me was up above and what was down below was just a body. I felt I was dead and there was nothing I could do about it.

Right after that, I saw my youngest brother Paul. He had been in a car accident the previous April, in which he was killed. He was a week short of 24 years old. That had torn the heart out of us. When I saw him, he was really there, exactly as I knew him. He was right beside me. We were in the same place, wherever that was. I had a conversation with him.

We had been really close and we used to have lots of

conversations. I used to be complaining that I was fed up with my job. He used to say, 'Well, what are you going to do about it?' It was like as if we were having one of those chats again. He was saying, 'How can we tell them you are gone as well?' He was really saying it would break their hearts at home if I was gone, too. I also think he was implying that I had a choice to go back. I think he was telling me to return.

At that stage, I saw my own funeral and I saw everyone's faces. He saw that, too. I saw I was being buried beside where my brother was. I was very upset because of that. I suddenly felt I had things to do and that I needed change in my life. I felt I had to come back and do things that were important to me. I felt, too, that if my parents lost two sons it would have been devastating.

Once I had that chat, I decided to come back. I made the decision. It was like I wasn't afraid anymore. The next thing, I was back in my body and lying on the ground. I had come to, although I wasn't able to talk. I knew I was alright then. One of the lads later told me that a woman had come along and was helping me at the time. She was wearing a miniskirt. They said that must have been why I responded so quickly! They were only joking.

The lads then brought me off to the hospital, which was nearby. I didn't have any burns or anything, although I was heavily traumatised. They checked me up and down. They then let me go. I think somebody brought my car over to the hospital and I drove home, although I was shattered and rattled by the whole experience. How I lived, I don't know. I had been in grave danger.

After the experience, I really believe something changed in my life. I had spent a lot of time before trying to please other people, but now I was going to follow my heart and do things for myself. And that's what I did. I got into other things and got into different work. I wasn't afraid any longer. I wasn't afraid of dying and I wasn't afraid of living either. Religion took a back seat. I stopped going to Mass, except on special occasions. I think I became more spiritual instead.

I also grew to know that people have been dying since time began, so it can't be that big a deal. I really think I'm not afraid of it, and when you're not afraid of it you can live. I feel that when it comes, it will come. People talk about the soul or the spirit and something that comes from within. I think that will eventually leave my body and float away. And when it does, I think I will meet my brother once again. I really believe he will be there and waiting.

CLAIRE, FROM COUNTY KERRY, encountered her dead son during a near-death experience.

We left for a holiday in Brazil on 31 December 2011. We had decided to stay there for a full three months, until the end of March. We wanted to go away somewhere where the sun was shining. I have suffered from anxiety in the past. My husband has suffered from depression. So we went there and immensely enjoyed the first month. We had a wonderful time.

At the end of the second month, my husband had a severe accident. It wasn't that severe in the sense of it being life-threatening. Instead, he fell down a last step, which he didn't see. He just sort of missed it. All his body weight came down on his right knee, pulling the tendons, ligaments and muscles from his leg.

I had to get him to a hospital, where he had an urgent operation. He was there for ten days. I needed to stay with him during that time. After he was discharged, he couldn't fly home because he had thrombosis, or coagulation of the blood, so we had to stay in a hotel for almost two months. Throughout this time, he couldn't move or walk. He couldn't go anywhere. I took care of him all that time.

After two months, we came back home to Ireland, to County Kerry. Before we left, I was very concerned about everything. I was particularly worried about the flight because of his thrombosis, which was still very dangerous. The travelling took about 30 hours and he was still in a lot of pain. We also had to get an ambulance for the last part of the journey. The whole thing was very stressful.

When we arrived home, in the first week of May, we were both exhausted and worn-out. I was particularly restless and nervous. I felt really uncomfortable and anxious and also very, very tired. I thought it was a backlash from the journey and the anxiety and pressure that I had gone through.

Less than a week later, I got very unwell. I stayed in bed for 36 hours because my body just couldn't handle things anymore. At one stage, I came downstairs from my bedroom to arrange something to eat. I was trying to give instructions to my husband about the cooking of the food. I planned that we would then bring the food back upstairs.

I remember saying to my husband to put the food in the microwave oven to let it cook. Unfortunately, at the time, everything was upside down in the house and he put the food, with two covers still on, into the microwave oven. The covers all melted into the meat. I said, 'Oh, my God! How did that happen?'

All of a sudden, I collapsed. My husband had to call for a neighbour to come over because he couldn't drive a car after his accident. After a while, the neighbour arrived. By this stage, I was back in bed, having been helped there by my husband. While there, I felt a very bad pressure in the breastbone. I felt really sick. I also felt pain in my left upper arm and my neck. My neighbour and my husband eventually drove me to hospital.

When I got there, they found that my blood pressure was very high. My heartbeat was very fast. I was sick and in a lot of discomfort. They put me on oxygen and gave me tablets. The next thing, I was unconscious. I had been lying down in bed at the time. Suddenly, everything became very peaceful. I'd had a heart attack and I was completely gone to the other side!

The first thing I saw was a very big, white light, the size of half a circle, down below my feet. I was looking down at it. It wasn't a tunnel with a light. Instead, it was an arc of light, like a full half-circle. It was very, very bright and it was in front of me. I wasn't blinded by it and it was very relaxing. I was attracted to it, but I wasn't going to it.

On both my left-hand and my right-hand sides was grass, along with beautiful little marigold flowers, white on the outside and yellow on the inside. The flowers weren't in bunches, but were well-organised. There was dew all over the grass. There was very soft music in the background. Everything was very peaceful. I was amazed.

Lying on the grass was my son. I had only one child and he had passed away when he was 18 years of age. He was a healthy, beautiful boy, but had died in February 1995 from a heart attack. He was on my right side, lying there. He was near my leg, just by my right knee. I saw his body, but not his feet. He was lying on the dew, with the green grass on either side of him. There was nobody else there apart from him.

He seemed to be content, peaceful and happy. He was very relaxed, with a smiling face, but he didn't say anything to me. He was sleeping. He wore this sweatshirt, which was a dark-blue marine colour. On the right-hand and left-hand sides of the sweatshirt was written 'Kappa', which was his favourite brand of clothes. It was also his favourite sweatshirt; he loved it.

Everything then faded away. It vanished very slowly, very gently and very easily. I then came back to consciousness. I don't know how many hours I had been gone: one, two, three or maybe more. When I woke up, the medical team were all around my bed and were coming and going. They were checking my heart rate, doing electrocardiograms and things like that. They were very busy and had been working on me all the time.

At first, I didn't realise what was going on. I was in a very low state. In fact, it took me a long time before I realised I'd had a heart attack. I couldn't take it all in. I also didn't remember what had happened regarding the light and my son. Even when it did come back to me, I told nobody. I was afraid that the doctors would think I was crazy.

Eventually, when I saw my specialist, I plucked up enough courage to open up about it. I told her exactly what had happened. She was looking straight at me. She said, 'It's not the first time I've heard this. It's a near-death experience you've been through.' I was really very shocked, as I hadn't thought of a near-death experience. She said, 'You were going to the other side.' When she told me that, I froze in the chair. That same day, in the evening, I told my husband.

I still feel that what happened was unbelievable. Every time I think of it, I see exactly the same image. It's a very peaceful image and I am amazed by that. It's in no way frightening; instead, it's very calming. It's also like, while I was there, my son was letting me know, 'Mom, I'm happy now!'

I absolutely believe I saw my son. He is at peace and very happy; happier even than when he was alive. I don't know where he is and I don't know whether or not it is heaven. Our image of heaven is very different from what I saw. But I definitely think he is in some place, a very bright place, a happy place where you live forever. I also think I will meet him again.

FRANK, FROM COUNTY LONGFORD, was met by welcoming deceased people during a near-death experience he had as a young boy.

In the summer of 1968, two of my brothers, a friend and I went down to a nearby building site. I was 14 years old at the time. I was the oldest of the four of us. There was a big hole in the ground there, which was about 20 feet around and maybe 15 feet deep. It was full of water. We used to throw stones in the water and generally mess around. We were warned never to go down there, but we did.

On this summer's day, we started throwing stones at the midges in the water. Because it was summer, the mud was very dry and flaky. My brother had a big, long stick and he was splashing the water with it. He was stooped down at the edge of the hole. I came up behind him, caught him by the shoulders and said, 'You're gone, only for I caught you!' He got such a fright that he sat down on the ground and started to cry.

I took about five steps away from him and the bank gave way under me. All the stones and the grit started to collapse away into the water. As I started to fall in, I turned around to grab onto something, but there was nothing there. My brothers were too far away to catch me, although they ran and tried to help.

Everything suddenly slowed down. Everything went into slow motion. It felt like it took me minutes to hit the water, although it probably only took me a fraction of a second. I hit the water, which was a lot colder than I was. I was struggling and was trying to grab onto something. I couldn't swim, so I started to go up and down.

My face would come up and I would get a breath and then go back down again. That happened between 15 and 20 times. The last time it happened, I instinctively knew I wasn't going to come back up. I could feel myself slowly floating down in the water. When I hit the bottom, I knew I was there because of the consistency of the mud. Everything then just went pitch-black.

Suddenly, everything came to life again and I felt I was sitting on a chair in the middle of a room. It was a big room. On the wall facing me, there was this sort of big projection screen. My whole life came up in colour and it was replayed in front of me. The colour was amazing. There were summer days, winter days, everything. I then saw myself falling into the water on the screen. Everything went black. I had come to the end of my life.

The next thing, I felt like I was in a tunnel and there was a light very far away. I felt like I was going down a tube towards the light. I was flying down the pipe, going really fast. There was no panic. I wasn't afraid. I went into the light. It wasn't like sunlight; instead, it was a matt light. I went through it and came out the other side. I felt I was standing on sand, either on a beach or in a desert. I really felt the place I was in was 'the light'. I felt enveloped by it.

I looked around and in front of me were about 25 or 30 people. They were standing around in a semicircle. Their lips were moving, so I knew they were all talking, although I couldn't hear any words or hear their voices. I couldn't hear what they were saying. I just knew they were there to greet me, although I didn't recognise any of them. I definitely knew they were there for me. They gave me a very warm welcome.

These people started to walk towards me. They looked like ordinary people and I knew they knew me. I knew I had some connection with them. I felt they were related to me in some way and I felt really wanted. I'm convinced they were my dead relations. They were wearing clothes not from 1968 but from a long time before that, maybe the early 1900s. Most of them were dressed in black, both women and men. I wasn't afraid of them in any way. Nobody said, 'It's not your time' or anything like that.

The next thing that came into my mind was the Act of Contrition. I wasn't breathing at this stage, so my mouth wasn't opening. But I was conscious and started to 'think' the Act of Contrition in my mind. I was halfway through it when I felt this hand on my back. It was the whole flat of a hand midway down my back. The hand lifted me up out of the hole, which I was in the middle of, and pushed me over to the embankment.

My friend and my two brothers pulled me out. They had been frozen with fright and couldn't believe I was after coming back up. We then went up to a field behind where the building work was going on. We lit a bonfire and dried my clothes. I didn't tell my mother what happened until I was 24. I think she might have brought me down and thrown me back in!

I have never forgotten what happened. Although I was only 14 at the time and it was a long time ago, it's like it only happened yesterday. I believe I was in another dimension, a different place, at the time. I think it's where we go when we die, some sort of continuation of life. Wherever that is, the light is everything. It was completely enveloping. I am firmly convinced that eventually I will be going back to that light and my parents will be there.

I am not religious, although I was at the age of 14. What I now feel is that there is only one thing in life and that's happiness. Happiness is family to me. I think other people's happiness is the most important thing. I think you have to do the best you can for them. I reared my children to be happy, nothing else. Money might be essential, but there are people who don't have much and they are happy. That's what I think we should all strive for in our lives.

CATHERINE, FROM COUNTY CORK, was reunited with dead relatives after she became seriously ill.

It was June 2005. I was in my 40s at the time. I was extremely healthy and fit, and I was about to do a sponsored walk overseas. I pulled a muscle in my back, but I was given muscle relaxants and I did the walk. I went on a holiday to Mexico in September. A week after returning, I got a sore throat. I then came out in blisters. I thought it was because of the holiday or chickenpox. Unfortunately, it wouldn't go away.

I was admitted to the hospital. A dermatologist eventually looked at my skin and took a swab. She felt it was something more sinister. She sent the swab off to another hospital and then had me sent up to the burns unit immediately. My skin was actually burning. It turned out to be a toxic reaction to a drug I was taking. It was very rare. There was only a one-in-a-million chance that I would get what I had and a one-in-four chance I could die.

I was critically ill and I was covered in cream and gauze. I couldn't be touched because my skin would blister. My family were called in and told how bad I was, that things were touch-and-go and that they didn't know what would happen. I remember thinking, 'My eldest daughter knows where my will is.' I also thought, 'There's enough money to bury me.'

Around that time, a strange incident happened. I was in my bed and I remember sitting up and I saw this light ahead of me. It was a soft light, like candlelight and not blinding. I was in a tunnel, like a passageway, and heading towards the light. It was getting brighter and brighter as I went along. I wasn't going at speed; I was more like floating. I didn't feel stressed or anything. It was lovely and I was at peace. It wasn't a fearful place at all.

At the end of the light, I spotted three people: my mother, my father and my brother. They all had passed away. They looked exactly the same as they were before they died. They hadn't aged. They were happier and not stressed like they used to be back in this world. Everyone, I suppose, has difficulties in this life, but they didn't have them in their world.

They were smiling at me, but they never said anything. I felt very happy, content and glad to see them. It was a really nice experience. Initially, I wanted to go to them. I felt that the reason I had sat up in the bed was to do just that. But I suddenly felt I wasn't ready.

I think I was about halfway when I felt I didn't want to continue. I thought, 'If I go down there, I'm not coming back.' I didn't want to leave because of my children and my husband. I also wasn't ready to leave this world, as I had more to do. So I stopped and looked at the three people ahead of me and I said, 'I'm not ready!'

I had one foot just beyond the halfway mark, but I didn't go any further. My right foot was suspended and I had to decide whether to step forward with it or not. Instead, I came back and back. My father, mother and brother started disappearing into the distance. They got smaller and smaller.

My body came back into the pillow. It was all a bit foggy after that, although it was just afterwards, according to my husband, that I started to get better. It was the turning-point in my recovery. I was back in contention to survive.

I was in hospital for a month and it probably took me six months to get better. I lost two stone in weight and I could barely walk. I wasn't eating or anything. They ultimately diagnosed the toxic drug reaction, but they couldn't name what drug was responsible. The net result is that I now have to be careful of taking any drugs and of the sun. It really was a serious illness.

It was only afterwards I wondered, 'Did this really happen or was it a dream?' I knew it was something different. It was something very spiritual. I'm sure I was near death at the time, probably 90 per cent dead, but something made me stop and say I wasn't ready. I also think my relatives were coming to welcome me to wherever they are. I think if I had put that one foot forward, I would have gone to them. But I chose to stay.

I'm sure I'll meet them again. Up to then, I wasn't sure where we go to when we die. Now, part of me believes that there is something afterwards and that you do go to another place. I haven't thought about that aspect of it very much, but I do think I will meet them again in heaven.

It changed my life after I returned. I'm very grateful to be alive and I'm grateful for what I have. I decided not to get caught up in the daily stresses and worries of life. I think what happened also told me that it was my time to focus on me, which I hadn't been doing up to that. I was working very hard and I was halfway through my life.

I felt that maybe I was now turning a corner and changing direction. It changed my view on working. It changed my view on people who had similar experiences. I gave more to others as a result, but I also gave more to myself. I thought, 'Your health is your wealth.' If you don't have it, you have nothing. All the money in the world isn't going to change that.

MARY, FROM COUNTY DOWN, met her husband's grandparents shortly after experiencing a medical emergency.

I lost a baby on New Year's night of 1995 into '96. A few nights after I miscarried, I was asleep in bed. I had been resting at home. For lack of a better word, I 'dreamed' that I met with my husband's grandparents. They came to me. His grandparents had died before I could meet them. I didn't know them, yet I knew who they were even though I had never seen them before.

They were in my downstairs hallway. It was as though I was welcoming them into my home. They didn't stay. It was as if they were saying, 'We're not coming in to stay.' It was only like I was meeting them. It also wasn't like I was going down a tunnel. It was more like they were coming to me, not that I was going to them.

They were dressed in clothes of their era. The grandfather was wearing some sort of serge-style gabardine coat. I later discovered it related to work he had done at one stage in his life. His wife wore a fawn-coloured raincoat and a coloured scarf.

The grandfather said to me, 'We've come for the parcel!' I gave them something wrapped up in a blanket. I then walked with them, as if I was seeing them to the door. The grandmother turned to me and said, 'You're not coming with us! It's not your time!' The grandfather said, 'Tell your husband that I will take care of this parcel until you come home!' They then went out my front door.

The next morning, when I woke, I said to my husband, 'I

had a strange dream last night. I met your grandparents.' He asked me, 'What was it about?' I said, 'Your grandfather told me to tell you that they would take care of the parcel until you come home.' Although I referred to what took place as a dream, it was different from that. I really felt I was there, in a different place. I was feeling and talking. I could see all around me. It wasn't just me looking at something; I was in the experience. So, I suppose, it genuinely was different from a dream.

My husband's mother lives not too far away from us. Later that day, he happened to be up with her. He hadn't told anyone at that stage about either my being pregnant or the miscarriage. He said to his mother, 'Mary was expecting a baby, but she has miscarried. She's resting and that's why she is not with me today.' His mother said, 'I've been dreaming about her and I prayed for her to my father last night.' It was strange how she was praying to her father around the same time as I had my dream.

About a week after it happened, I was given a gift which included a photograph of the grandfather. It was exactly as I had seen him. The grandfather was the only one of the two grandparents in it. He was working in the garden. The image of him coming to me in the hallway was identical. I saw a photograph of the grandmother, years later, and she was the same, too.

Because of what had happened, I had to be admitted to hospital. I had to have surgery. It was a difficult time, but what had occurred gave me a lot of consolation. I had grown to love the baby and I had plenty of hopes and dreams. Although I had lost the baby, I now had a sense of where it had gone. I felt we would meet again and that helped me a lot.

The experience of losing the baby was an eye-opener to

me. People talk of mothers and children dying in childbirth. I thought, 'That only happened years ago.' But I could have very easily died in the circumstances and my baby did die. I was lucky to have lived. So it did take me a long time to get over it emotionally.

I believe that life is a continuum. Those who have passed before us live on. Jesus said he would go and prepare a place for us, and where he is we will be, too. I believe that our child is with his great-grandparents and that, wherever they are, they will be looking after the baby. There, in that place, we will all meet again.

JACKIE, FROM COUNTY DUBLIN, was greeted by her dead grandparents in the aftermath of a difficult childbirth.

I gave birth to my son Séamus back in 1990. I had to have a Caesarean section. Giving birth the natural way would have been too dangerous. Neither of us would have been here today if we had gone that route, according to the surgeon. Everything turned out grand in the end. The baby was healthy, thank God.

A couple of days afterwards, I was still in the hospital and feeling very sore and tired. I was resting in my bed in the ward. Suddenly, I found myself floating up out of my body. I found myself in a tunnel, like the sort that cars would go through. It was very wide. It would have taken me maybe ten or 15 minutes to walk through it, but I was floating along at medium speed.

There was a bright, dazzling light throughout the tunnel. It was a white light, like the colour of a tin of the brightest paint, maybe even brighter. The light was all over the place. Really, the tunnel was made of light. I was wondering where I was and where I was going to. I didn't know what was happening. I felt disbelief. I didn't know what I was doing. I was just worried about what was at the end of this journey.

I suddenly came to the end of the tunnel, where there was this beautiful garden. The grass was so green. On the left, three angels were playing harps and singing. The music was gorgeous. To the right of the garden was this grey stone house with a brown door. It was like a church, but it really was a mansion. It looked medieval. The sky was blue and the sun was shining.

After that, my grandparents came out of the house and they met me at the edge of the tunnel. They had died back in the 1970s. My grandfather had died of throat cancer; my grandmother from lung cancer. They were both big smokers. I loved them very much and had gone to visit them a lot.

They looked very well and were floating around like me. They were wearing white robes and looked the same age as they were before they died. They also looked really healthy and happy. There was no sickness or worry or tension. They told me they were well looked after and well fed. They were very happy to see me and they gave me a big hug.

My grandparents then said they would have driven to the hospital in their car to see the baby, but they had died back in the 1970s. I was amazed to hear them saying that. They said they were delighted my son was born. They told me to look after him and to look after myself.

I was just so surprised by what was after happening. I was happy, too. I wanted to go into the house with them, but they said it wasn't my time and that I should go back and take care of my son. I was a bit disappointed, but I knew I had to return and look after Séamus. It was my job.

They also said that meeting me at the end of the tunnel was their one and only chance to meet me for now. They said they would see me again when it was my turn to go, but that was a long way away yet. After that, they gave me a hug and

I started going back through the tunnel again. They went into the house, which I think was God's house in heaven.

I floated down and I came back inside myself. The next thing, I woke up, but I couldn't move. There was this cardiac machine there and I was all strapped in, with wires coming out of me and extending across my mouth. I really couldn't move. It was like I was nailed down. They were resuscitating me. I heard later that my heart had stopped and they were trying to get me back.

I felt thrilled later on when I thought about what had happened. I had been close to my grandparents and it was great to see them. I had been with them shortly before they died. We got on very well. I would be with them most weekends. That had gone on for a couple of years. So I was very happy to meet up with them once more.

I know I will meet my grandparents again. My parents are also dead and I will meet them, too. I think they will all be waiting for me. It's a gorgeous place that they are in, and I know that's where I will be going when I die. However, as my grandparents said, my death is a long way away yet and, at the moment, I'm in no hurry to go.

PADDY, FROM COUNTY CORK, met deceased relatives, among others, after he 'died' for a short time during a serious operation in 2009.

I had a bypass and a valve replaced in my heart back in 2009. It was a serious operation, which took place on the shortest day of the year, 21 December. I had been in the hospital for three weeks beforehand. Earlier on, I had problems indicating that something was wrong. I was very slow going up hills. I would be caught for breath. It wasn't like it used to be.

The operation was long and complicated. During it, I met every one of my family who had passed away beforehand. I met my father and mother. My mother had died in 1976, at the age of 76. My father was buried when I was only five years old. I am in my later 70s now, so he died over 70 years ago.

I recognised my mother straight away. She had been a fairly tall, hardworking woman, who had been left without a husband and had to manage a small farm. She was always very busy, baking and so on. She never had much money. I saw her clearly, moving around and looking at me.

My father was sitting down in a chair. He was dressed in his ordinary clothes. I presume that was the way he always dressed, but I don't remember because, as I mentioned, he died when I was five. This young fellow was beside him, who was also fully dressed. I immediately guessed that the young person was a brother I had never seen. He was only ten years old when he died from meningitis. At that time, there was no cure for it.

My brother's name was John and I never met him because I was born after him. I'm sure it was him. It must have been. I had seen him in a picture and it looked like him. He also looked exactly the same as one of my sons. They were almost identical.

My father-in-law was there, too, exactly the same as when I knew him. He was dressed in his working clothes. All of them were scattered in different places, yet they weren't too far away from each other. They weren't far from me either. They were all looking at me and were happy, but they weren't smiling. In fact, they were quite serious and no words were spoken.

There were lots of different people there, but I couldn't recognise most of them. Some were sitting and more were just moving around. One of those I recognised was Pope John Paul II. I had great time for him, and I went up to

Limerick to see him when he came to Ireland. He was sitting in his chair, a good bit away from me, as real as could be. He was dressed in his robes and had a brownish cape thrown over his shoulders. He was a beautiful man and had a grand way about him. He also had that look when I saw him.

There was no sky in the place where I saw my relatives. It seemed to be inside somewhere. It looked like they were all in some big room, like a kitchen. I couldn't make out where it was. The Pope was in a different place, which was much brighter. A light shone on him. He looked very radiant. I was really happy to see them all and I didn't want to come back.

The operation was a success. When I woke up, it hit me, 'Where was I?' I think at that time I was as good as dead. The doctor later told me I had died for some time. They had machines keeping me alive. I'm certain that, during that time, what I had wasn't just a dream. Instead, I'm really convinced I was in heaven and I was happy to be there.

Although I really don't know all the answers, I'm sure that when we die we will meet our relatives who passed on before us. I have often seen people dying and I have no doubt that in the last few seconds someone comes to meet them. I have seen their eyes open and they smiled as they looked at the ceiling. I have witnessed this before.

It's not that I'm very religious, although I always say a few prayers especially before I go to bed at night. But I do believe there is something there. For example, the morning when I went in for the operation, I invited Padre Pio, St. Anthony and the Holy Spirit in with me. The whole thing was complicated and lasted a long time. Yet, when I woke, I put my hand on my chest because I thought the operation wasn't done at all. I hadn't any pain or any ache or any soreness. The only thing I had was a big thirst. Otherwise, I was perfect. It was amazing.

I often think about what happened and I now get really annoyed with people who say there is no next world. I believe – and I will believe until the day I die – that I will be facing into that next world after I pass away. I also have no doubt whatsoever that I will see my relatives again. I will meet all those who passed before me. They will come to meet me and welcome me. The day of hard work will be gone and it will be a very happy place. I'm sure of that.

SHEILA, WHO COMES FROM COUNTY TYRONE but who now lives in the UK, was reunited with her deceased grandfather during an out-of-body experience.

When I was about three-and-a-half, I felt unwell. This was back in the early 1940s. I was extremely hot and then I was cold. All of a sudden, I was out of my body. I looked back on the bed and I was there. I then went out through a sash-window, which was half open, and I travelled away.

All of a sudden, I was in a very nice place. Not only was it bright, but it was full of flowers. There was a lovely feeling about it. It was gorgeous. The light was very bright, but not glaring. I went towards it. The trip was lovely, quick and nice and not frightening.

There was a man there, with brightness around him. I said to him, 'Are you God?' He said, 'No, I'm Grandfather Baxter!' He was a grandfather of mine who had died a couple of weeks before I was born. He had a moustache and he was smiling at me. He had a tweed coat on him, with a flower attached to his lapel, and he looked nice. He said, 'You can't come in here yet! You can't come in here until you are as old as Granny!'

I eventually came back to my body. I was then telling my mother what happened and that I had seen Granddad. She was in awe of it. I kept asking her what age Granny was when she died, but she never told me. She just kept saying, 'She was old.' I later looked for Granny's gravestone in the graveyard, but they had smashed it down. The local church had built an extension to a hall and got rid of it. So I never saw her age, although she would definitely have been well into her 70s.

It happened again when I was 26 years old and married. My husband was away at the time and I was staying with my mother. We had a sash-window in the house and it was summertime. It was half open. All of a sudden, I got a feeling in my chest as if somebody had got a strap and pulled it tightly. I was trying to breathe, but I couldn't. I called for help and tried to get out of bed, but I couldn't move.

The next thing, I shot out of my body. I was again headed out through a sash-window. I saw a bright light and I was going towards it. I then looked back and I was lying there with my long hair and my mouth and eyes open. It scared me at the time. I think if I hadn't looked back, I would have gone to the light.

Instead, I thought, 'If my mother comes in during the morning, it's going to kill her.' The reason I thought that was because a brother of mine had died a few months before. So, all of a sudden, I was back in my body and trying to breathe again. Eventually, I was fine, although the next day I was so tired and so unwell I couldn't get out of bed. I was extremely exhausted and weak.

I never found out what was wrong that time and I have no idea what happened. What I do know, however, is that I brought something back from the other side and I have been psychic ever since. Afterwards, I could see things that other people couldn't see and I have known things that I shouldn't have known. I can see the future. I could have been a fortune-teller, if I wanted to, but I never wanted to do it except for helping a few friends who had problems.

I really think I was passing away at the time of the first experience and I was at the gates of heaven. I now know it's a bright and beautiful and peaceful place. As a result, I've never been afraid about death since. I'm spiritual now and I am a better person. I go to Mass and I don't harm anyone. I wouldn't even kill a fly. Everything is allowed to live in my garden. I also believe in God and I believe that there is a heaven which is peaceful and gorgeous. It's there alright.

WILLIAM, WHO LIVES IN COUNTY CORK, describes how his deceased wife came to him as he lay dying after a near-tragic fall.

I had an accident where I fell from a very high roof. I was very lucky because my fall was cushioned. Otherwise, I would almost certainly have died. After I fell, I saw the light. It was a blinding light at the end of a tunnel which I was going through. The light went on and off. I was sure I was dying.

I could see a person standing about ten feet away. It was a woman and she was on her own. She was on my right-hand side, standing in the corner of the room on the wood floor. She looked slim, was dressed in a grey coat and her hair was grey. Her outline was real and she looked like a real person.

I thought it was my wife, who had already passed away. She had died some time before from breast cancer, which had spread to her lymph glands and throughout her body. The person standing there looked exactly as she did at the time she had died, with the same face and hands. The coat was also the same coat that she always wore.

She was worried-looking and was obviously concerned, but she never moved and just stood there, always on my right-hand side, without coming over to me. Her hands stayed still and she was completely motionless. All she did was look at me and stare at me. Her head never moved, nor her eyes or arms or anything else.

She never said anything to me. I didn't say anything to her either. When I think back on it, I find it odd that I said nothing. In fact, the whole thing seemed strange. She just stayed there the whole time. Eventually, the other lads I was working with arrived and got me to hospital. It was only then that she disappeared.

I had an earlier accident, which was a car crash, but no one came to me then. I was going to work early one morning on a dual carriageway and the next thing this car came flying across the road barrier at me. The car came straight for me, doing about 90 miles an hour. The driver had fallen asleep.

The engine of my car came in on top of me. The seat I was sitting on was broken off and I went backwards. I had a passenger with me in the car and he had to get 40 stitches in his face. The windscreen was gone and the car was a write-off. My ears were full of glass and I'm sure I had swallowed some as well. But nobody appeared to me that time. Maybe that was because my wife was alive at that stage, although I suppose I had other dead relatives who could have come to me, but they didn't.

Looking back at the time I fell from the roof, I'm sure it was my wife that I saw. I really believe she came to me to meet me. I thought maybe she was there because, as my wife, she had arrived to protect me and mind me. I felt happy that she was with me and making sure that I was alright, even though she was just standing there.

I believe people come to us when we are dying. I think they arrive to help us and to guide us to the other side. I also believe that when I eventually die, my wife will come to me again and that we will meet someday. I hope other relatives appear to me, too. But that day of the fall, I am sure it was her. I really believe she was looking after me, taking care of me and helping me to survive.

JODIE, FROM COUNTY WEXFORD, has three stories to relate: one concerning her grandparents; two others involving her mother.

Approximately 30 years ago, I had an operation. It was for gallstones. Initially, my doctor kept telling me there was nothing wrong, but I ended up in Emergency. I had a very hard time in hospital and I had to be admitted to Intensive Care. The whole thing was very tough on me.

During my stay in hospital, I had a strange experience. I didn't see bright lights or anything. There was no tunnel. Instead, I was walking on this road. It was a long road, with a couple of curves to it. They weren't full corners, just gentle curves.

The road was like a creamy-white Tarmac. I was aware of fields on each side of it. Although they had no boundaries, I still knew they were small, individual fields. I was looking either side of me and I definitely could make them out, yet there were no hedgerows.

I was walking behind my grandmother and my grandfather. They were dead at this stage. They were linking each other, which they never did in real life. They weren't walking fast, just ambling or strolling. It was like they were having a conversation. They had their backs to me. I was trying to catch up with them, but I couldn't catch my breath. I was trying really hard, yet I couldn't get to them.

They walked on ahead until they came to a corner, which went to the right. There was a high wall to the left of the corner, but I don't know what was behind it or what it signified. It was an old wall and it looked like it was made of stone. That wall was to their left and I think there was a low hedge to their right.

My grandmother suddenly turned around and said to me, 'Go back! You're not to follow us! Go back!' They then went around the corner and I couldn't see them anymore. I really don't know what happened after that. I suppose I just woke up at some stage.

Later on, when my mother was very ill, I nursed her for a long time. She had bowel cancer. She came to live with me in our house and we turned our sitting-room into a bedroom for her. When she was dying, she kept calling out all these different names. I would be sitting up with her at night and she would be going through this litany of people. It was very strange, but she was clearly in touch with them from elsewhere.

I also believe my mother had an out-of-body experience before she died. One night, I was reading in my bed when I suddenly became aware that someone had floated into my room. I sat up and saw my mother. She had a grey coat on her, which she used to have years and years ago. She was facing towards the wall at the foot of the bed. She then turned around and looked straight at me.

After that, she was gone. I got an awful fright and said, 'Something has happened to Mammy!' I thought she had died. I jumped out of the bed and ran around the end of the bed and out the door, into her room. She was awake and she said to me, 'Was I just in your bedroom?' I couldn't believe it. I think it must have been an out-of-body experience that she had.

Looking back, I can't say what caused these experiences and I don't fully know what they were. But I am certain it was my grandmother and it really was her voice. I recognised it because I used to spend a lot of time with her as a child. I would go up to visit her on a Sunday or I would carry her shopping home with her on a Friday. I'm sure it was her.

Although I regularly think about what happened, I don't believe it transformed my life. I sometimes worry that people might think I'm a little weird. As a result, I don't tell many people. But, as I said, I'm sure my mother was in contact with the people she was identifying before she died, and I believe it really was my grandparents I saw that time when I was sick. To this day, I can still hear my grandmother's voice telling me to go back.

MARTINA, WHO COMES ORIGINALLY FROM COUNTY LAOIS but who lives in Surrey in the UK, was visited by her deceased grandmothers.

I was raised in a cottage out in the country. It was a basic cottage, with a kitchen-cum-sitting-room and a scullery out the back. There were 14 in the family: seven boys and seven girls. The cottage had three bedrooms: the parents' room, the boys' room and the girls' room. I was sleeping in the girls' bedroom.

I went into the girls' bedroom one day. It was a very small room, just off the kitchen-cum-sitting-room. The door opened inwards and the bed was behind it. The wall behind the door was the connecting wall to the kitchen. Up high on that wall was a shelf and there was a live bulb socket there as well. In effect, the bulb socket was on the wall rather than in the ceiling.

I was quite inquisitive and I stood up on the end of the bed to reach the live socket on the wall. I put my finger into it. I have no idea why I did it, maybe because we were doing something about electricity at school. I was aged around six or eight at the time. I remember I went shooting across the room and fell straight back into the bed.

The next thing, I saw a lovely lady sitting beside the bed and smiling at me. She was a small old lady, with silver hair and wearing black silk. There was a rustling sound from her skirt. She just sat there beside the bed while I drifted in and out. There was a kind of musty smell from her, which was very strong. Although I associated the smell with the black silk, it must have been mothballs that I smelled from her.

My mother eventually came into the room. She must have heard the bang. I might have screamed out as well. I told her that she didn't have to worry about me and I described the nice lady who had been sitting beside me. I told her about everything, including the rustle of the skirt. It turned out that the old lady I had seen was my paternal grandmother. She had died way before I was born.

My mother left the room after that and I think there was whispering outside. She must have told my father what I said. Eventually, he came in and I can remember him sitting beside my bed. Coming into my bedroom was something he would normally never do. He must have been very curious about his mother. He seemed fascinated by what I had seen and asked me again to describe the lady who had been sitting beside me. I told him about her.

I know definitely that the person I had seen was my granny and I think she had come back to me. I believe she knew that while I had put my hand in a socket and may have faced death, it wasn't my time to go. I also think she has always been with me through my life.

I saw my mother's mother one time as well. It was in broad daylight. There was an old house which had been knocked down and turned into an open barn. A newer house had been built nearby. I saw an old lady sitting on the stoop of the old building, doing something with her hands. I can remember telling my sister that I had seen the old lady. She didn't even blink. She just said to me, 'Describe her.'

I described her and said I thought it was our maternal grandmother, who had also died long before. My sister asked me, 'What was she doing?' I immediately said, 'Knitting.' But my sister responded, 'She never did that. She never knitted.' I thought about it and came back to my sister about half an hour later and said to her, 'She was shelling peas.' My sister said, 'That's what granny did. She sat on the stoop in the evening and she shelled peas.'

I also have no doubt that the old lady was my maternal grandmother, although I don't know why she came to me at that time. I believe it was more to do with my sister. I think it was around the time that she had lost a baby. I think my granny's arrival was more as a comfort for her and to ensure that I would pass the message on. My sister definitely got solace from it.

I believe that spirits are all around us. They are non-body entities and are different from ghosts. A spirit is a loving presence. To me, they are an energy and eternal. They are with us day and night. I think that's what my grandparents who had appeared to me were – spirits. In contrast, there is a negative connotation to ghosts, which are really imprints of people who once travelled the earth or touched it.

I think it is spirits who come to us in our hour of need. They are alongside us every step of the way; it's just that we don't realise it. I think that the reason we don't see them is because we build up our own barriers. I believe we see them at times of crisis because some part of us cries out in despair. But I believe they are always there, without a doubt.

OTHER VISITATIONS

In the course of writing this book, many people either contacted me or came to my attention regarding other strange visions or visitations they experienced around the time of their loved ones' deaths. Most of the phenomena they reported seemed unrelated, at least directly, to the standard deathbed vision, where the person who is dying sees deceased relatives or friends.

Instead, many of the accounts described visits from afar from the dying or recently dead. They also involved strange forewarnings, vivid dreams, physical sensations, inexplicable lights and a range of other variations around these themes.

At first, these narratives seemed to be so unrelated to the subject-matter of this book – the deathbed vision – that I felt they should be excluded. Some cursory research, however, established that this course of action would be unwise. Scattered throughout historic texts, I found many examples supporting the case for their inclusion in a separate chapter.

Many of the stories I found date back a remarkably long way. Accounts where healthy people shared in their ailing relatives' deathbed visions were chronicled by the Society for Psychical Research in Britain as far back as the end of the nineteenth century. In one case, two sisters who were in attendance while another sister was dying observed a bright light containing the faces of two of their deceased brothers. The sister died soon after.

Other instances, where those who are dying appear to

relatives living at a distance, have regularly been recorded. Sometimes, the dying may report to those who sit with them where they have been and who they have seen. One example, dating back to the late seventeenth century, involved a woman named Mary Goffe, who was dying at her father's house some distance from her own home where her two children resided.

Mary expressed a great desire to visit her children, which due to her illness proved to be impossible. Between one and two o'clock at night, she was seen to fall into a trance. At exactly the same time, a likeness of her was spotted in her home observing her offspring while asleep. The following day, she declared to her mother that she had indeed visited her children the previous night. She died shortly afterwards.

In more up-to-date times, Dr. Raymond Moody – pioneer investigator of the near-death experience in the 1970s – chronicled multiple deathbed case histories where entire families described how they, too, had witnessed strange events at the time of a family member's death. Some outlined how they accompanied their loved ones on at least part of their afterlife journeys. Others described how they shared in the life reviews of those who were passing on. The following chapter features examples of at least some of the phenomena described above.

MAUREEN, FROM COUNTY LIMERICK, is convinced she was contacted by a friend who died. The event happened in 2010.

Back in the early 1960s, there was a lovely family from County Westmeath who came to our area to work. There was a young couple and their brothers, too. There was a big circle of family members around. Locals were friendly with them.

My family were close to them as well, although I never got to know them because I was only about seven or eight at the time. Eventually, they moved back to Westmeath.

In time, about 23 years ago, a neighbour of ours got the telephone in and decided to make contact with them. As a result, they decided to come down to visit. When they did, they stayed in our house. I was delighted because they were household names to me. It was great to meet them and to get to know them. They continued to visit over the years. We would go up to visit them, too. This went on for about 12 years or more, but then it stopped. We lost contact a bit after that.

One day, back in 2010, I was in one of the bedrooms in our house and was doing the usual jobs tidying it up. I was dressing the bed and things like that. All of a sudden, a feeling came over me that a person was connecting with me. I was being given the feeling that the person was very fond of me and was telling me that they were at peace.

The feeling was one of love. It felt like the person was hugging me. I felt very warm. Although there were no words spoken, I felt the spirit was saying that it was very happy with me. The immediate thought I had was, 'Somebody who stayed in this room has died!' but I didn't know who the person was.

Some days later, I got a smell like incense in the room. It was like the smell you would get at Mass or at a religious ceremony. I got it elsewhere in the house as well. I became a bit nervous as a result. It was only around then – that couple of days later – that it dawned on me that it had something to do with one of the people from Westmeath. The person who sprang to my mind was a really nice woman. I realised that she had slept in that bedroom when she came to visit. I made the connection.

I think her visits to us had meant a lot to her. We had a friendship and got on well. I always felt she had wanted to stay for longer but, for some reason, she had always been prevented from doing so. She had also been very good to us when we went up to visit them in Westmeath. She would invite us to her house and go all out to cook a lovely meal. There had been a special connection. I just knew she had died, and I knew it was she was the person who visited me in the room.

I thought, 'I'd better ring her family.' Unfortunately, the phone number of the people had been changed. But I rang the post office and they gave me the proper number. I then rang the family and was told that one of them, the exact same woman, who was then about 70 years old, had died. She had died around the time I had the feeling in the room. I was shocked to hear this.

I was eventually advised by a spiritual healer to sprinkle holy water in the bedroom and to say a prayer. I was also advised to open the window and to release the spirit. She believed that the spirit lives on and that I had to release it. That's what I did, and that's what I achieved. I never smelled the incense or felt the presence again.

To me, it was an amazing experience. Nothing like it has ever happened to me before or since. I think about it a lot and I told the woman's sister-in-law. She wasn't surprised and told me that she had similar experiences when her father passed away. So it does happen. And I think it was because I was close to the woman that she came to me at the time she died.

MARTIN, FROM WATERFORD CITY, describes a most peculiar occurrence that took place within seconds of his mother's death.

My mother was 88 years of age and she was in and out of hospital for weeks before she died. In her last years, she had developed brittle bones and they had started to break. Her hips had started to break, too. She then got a turn, where she started to go weak, and she had to be hospitalised. I knew about two days before she went into the hospital that she wouldn't be coming out again. I said it to my wife. I got a weird feeling about it.

She wasn't in hospital long when the doctor told me, 'She has cancer. It is in and around where the lungs are. We could operate, but she is very old.' My wife and I had to make a decision and I said to the doctor, 'No, there's no point putting her through that sort of hardship at her age.' They wondered whether they should tell her about the cancer and again I said, 'No, there's no point.'

Initially, she was in a general ward. She was then put into a ward which held people who were mostly dying of cancer. It was a quieter ward and there was very little traffic passing by. The advantage was that you could go in at any time and visit, so you could spend time there. Unfortunately, very few people came out of it.

A few hours before she died, the hospital put her into a separate room where she could be on her own and where people could gather around her. There were between 12 and 14 of us in there, including my wife and children and other people who had looked after her where she had lived. The priest was there, too.

We were all sitting down and talking and watching my mother, who was sleeping and just drifting away. We were positioned around her bed. I had my back to the door, which was one of those swinging doors. It was a double door and was very solid. In effect, I was standing between my dying mother and the door. My wife was on one side of me and my daughter was on the other.

Eventually, the nurse came in and examined my mother and said, 'The breaths are getting very short. She hasn't long left.' The priest started saying prayers and we joined in. We could see that she was going. I remember hearing her last breath. It was very peculiar to see her breathing, then sinking back and her last breath coming out. She was gone.

Suddenly, this gush of wind came past me. It was very strong and fast. It sounded like a 'whoosh'. It went right past me, hit the door, opened it and closed it again. The door literally flew open and closed; the wind was that strong. I was towards the door, away from my mother, and I could feel the gush going by. It was like as if someone walked out, pushed the door outwards and then came back in again.

Everybody looked around at the door. I did, too. They all heard the noise of the door opening and shutting and they were wondering why. Nobody said anything; nor did I. I think everybody thought, 'I'll say nothing because people will think I'm cracking up.' I also looked up at the priest and he looked at me. I know he saw what had happened, but he never said anything.

That door had never moved at any other time when we were there, except when people came in or went out. You would really have to push it to open it. You would have to put your hand to it and give it a good shove. The room also was in the middle of the hospital, where there were no winds and no draughts. Yet the door had opened out a good way, between two and three feet. It had just flipped open and had come back in again.

I thought everybody there had felt the wind, but it seems they had not. Even my wife hadn't noticed it, although she had seen the door open. It seems the wind had come out between my daughter and myself and hit the door. It had come between the two of us and no one else had felt it.

The moment was very brief. Because my mother had died, the whole place then got kind of upset. Prayers were said. As a result, the whole thing was forgotten about and everybody concentrated on my mother in the bed.

However, my daughter, who had been standing beside me, later said to me, 'Did you feel what I felt? Did you feel that wind passing by?' I said, 'I did.' 'I felt it, too,' she said. 'Thank God!' I replied. 'I thought I was the only one.' Nobody else said anything, even though they had seen what happened to the door.

They say that is what happens when the spirit departs. I have read that it occurs in a lot of cases, where people feel a wind or a breeze as the spirit emerges out of the body. They also say that it takes a few seconds for the soul to depart. It is said to take maybe five or ten seconds before it moves. It took that sort of time in my mother's case, too.

From what I have read, they also say that it is out through the top of the head and out through the ceiling that the soul is supposed to travel. But I'm not sure of that. When people come to collect you, they are mostly standing at the foot of your bed and they take you and move away. So there really is no basis for saying that deceased relatives arrive, or the soul travels away, in any particular direction.

I believe that what I had witnessed was my mother's spirit departing her body and travelling away. Something definitely went past me and out the door. I'm sure that was her soul departing. I have no doubt whatsoever. I also feel that what happened was directed at me. Maybe that was because I was her only child.

I am also sure that what happened with my mother will happen to me. I'm sure not everyone would believe that. You will always find sceptics and you would nearly have to bring them to the other side and show them before they would believe you. But I'm the kind of person who says, 'Show me and I'll believe it.' And I have witnessed it for myself.

EILEEN, WHO COMES ORIGINALLY FROM COUNTY KERRY but who resides in Dublin, explains what happened when her half-brother's wife died. She relates the story because her half-brother is now in his early 90s and suffering from deafness.

This story concerns my half-brother, John, who is based in Coventry. He was born to my mother as part of her first family. Eventually, her husband died and she married again. I am part of her second family. He is a very down-to-earth person, an ex-Irish Army man and very strong and solid in many ways. He is very practical and not easily susceptible or given to fanciful ideas. That's the primary reason why I was struck by what he told me.

John began his working life in Kerry as a coffin-maker. He was only about 16 years old at the time. Eventually, he and his brother joined the Irish Army and stayed there for some years. After he left the army, he moved to Coventry, where he worked as a cabinet-maker. He was a very good worker and was in the same job for years.

He met Clare, his future spouse, at one of the Irish dances over there. She was a nurse from County Carlow. They got a house and settled down. They were very close and had a very happy marriage, which lasted for 52 years. He loved her very much. She really was the love of his life.

She was, however, 11 years younger than he was, which is a fair gap. As a result, he always thought he would die before her. She thought that, too. She was afraid of him dying first. She spoke to me about it. She really did not want that to happen. I think she had a fear about it. I suppose that was part of their closeness.

A couple of years ago, we spent a holiday with them down in County Kerry. We rented a house there. We took them around to places that he wanted to see. We took him to where he had pitched camp while in the army. We took him to where he had worked in his first job as a coffin-maker. He actually met an old lady there of his vintage, who remembered the place he had worked in and he was delighted with that. He reminisced and they both loved the trip. It was a bit like a pilgrimage.

Unfortunately, shortly after they returned to England, his wife contracted leukaemia. She was in her mid-70s. She had been complaining of a pain in her back, but it turned out to be leukaemia. It was terminal and there was nothing anyone could do. Within about six months, she passed away. My step-brother was very badly hit by the whole thing.

As Clare was a nurse, she knew what was happening. The one thing she said was that she didn't want to die alone. That was her biggest fear. At first, she was at home and nurses were coming in, but towards the end she had to go into hospital. It was an uncomfortable time.

The week she died, John spent a lot of time with her. He was with her day after day. His daughters, one of whom lives in Coventry and the other in London, were there as well. The

London-based daughter had come up. If he wasn't there, one of them was there in the hospital.

Obviously, he wasn't young at that stage. Because of that, his daughters said to him, 'Go home. You need to get some sleep. You are exhausted.' They pressed him to go home because they were afraid for him and worried that he might collapse. He eventually gave in and they took him back to his house. The two daughters then went back to the hospital, while he said he would be in the next morning.

That night, after he had arrived back home, he turned off the bedroom light and went straight into bed. He was totally exhausted and drifted off to sleep. Suddenly, with the room still in darkness, he was woken up. He had not been long asleep. When he woke, he saw a light. He described it as a 'shimmery light.' And there was his wife, surrounded by the light, and she was smiling at him!

She was just beside his bed. He always slept with his hand out over the bedclothes because the hand would regularly go numb if he slept on it. This time, he felt his hand was being clasped. Whether that had woken him or not, he wasn't sure. But he was sure it was Clare and he wanted to talk to her.

He struggled upwards in the bed so that he could see her properly, hold her and speak to her. She seemed very happy and he wasn't frightened or anything. But she was only there for a short time and then she disappeared. The whole thing didn't last long.

He rang the hospital after that. They told him that Clare had died just at the time that he had seen her. He wasn't frightened by what they had said, but he was astonished. It hadn't been a frightening experience; instead, it was a happy one. He was especially glad that she had been happy and was letting him know that. He was comforted, especially when he thought about it later on.

I don't know what to think about it. I had one experience like it myself. Way back, I lost a son with cystic fibrosis. My husband, the little boy and I were sitting in the front room of a flat. The flat was up in the top of the house and the landlady was a very elderly lady and living downstairs.

We were talking when suddenly there was a very definite knock at the door. You couldn't mistake it for anything else. Everyone heard it. It was a knock that went on three times. I automatically went and opened up the door, but there was nobody there.

I ran quickly down the stairs to see if it was the landlady who knocked, even though I knew it couldn't have been because she was elderly and had arthritis. She was sitting at her table downstairs. I asked her if she had knocked and she said she hadn't. Strangely, our little son was diagnosed with cystic fibrosis soon after. I have never forgotten it.

I have, as a result, an open mind regarding events like the one that happened to my half-brother. Not only do I absolutely believe him, but I think there is more out there than we can physically see. Some people are probably more sensitive than others to events like these. And, although the two I described are the only things that happened to me or my family that I know of, I certainly wouldn't be a disbeliever.

KATHLEEN, FROM COUNTY FERMANAGH, has seen visions of people at the time of, or before, their deaths.

The first experience took place in the late 1970s. I was 28 years of age at the time. It involved my sister, who was four years younger than me and who was living away. We had got married in the same year and a year later she had a baby. It was in very delicate health when it was born. One Sunday evening, when it was three months old, my sister brought the baby up to the house. I was admiring how big it had got. She then left to go home.

The following day, all the rest of the family were having dinner. It was around one o'clock. My father was there along with my mother and brother. Another sister was home from England with her husband and children and they were there also. They were all eating dinner in the main house. But I wasn't with them. Instead, I was standing in an old barn that was joined on to the house. I was just looking around.

While I was out in the barn, suddenly my sister who had visited the previous day appeared to me. It was like she was in a picture about half the size of a door. She seemed to be physically there. She was roaring crying, looking for help. She was holding her baby with one hand and crying at the same time. She was most upset. She was shouting, 'Help! Help!' like she was in distress.

I felt sick to my stomach. It was like something evil had struck me. I suppose the feeling lasted about two minutes. I then decided to forget all about it and pretend it never happened. I walked out of the barn and went back into the house. We had no telephone at the time, so I couldn't ring her. Instead, I said to my brother, 'Is there any way we can go to our sister? I think she's in bad trouble.' But he said the car wasn't available because my sister from England was about to go off with her family and my mother for a drive.

About two hours later, a knock came to the door and my uncle was there. He brought us bad news. He said that my sister's house had gone on fire and the baby was burnt to death. My sister had tried to get to the baby but couldn't. I was badly shocked. I think I had some sort of vision that warned me of what was going to take place. That was the first time this sort of thing occurred.

A second example concerned my mother. It happened on a Wednesday, when she was lying in bed, dying. She was only 68 years of age, but had been sick for two years with a heart complaint and she also had suspected cancer, although they never opened her up to find out. I went into another room to clean it up because I knew she was going to die and I wanted to prepare it for a wake.

Suddenly, my mother appeared right in front of me. She was like she was in real life, the same height and wearing a green cardigan and a grey-and-black dress. She was smiling, with her arms folded and her hair permed. She didn't look sick at all. I got no big shock or anything. I just walked out of the room. She died the following Sunday. I always think that was a warning that she was going to go off to the next place.

A third example concerned an uncle of mine, who lived in County Cavan. He had kidney failure and he was up in Beaumont Hospital in Dublin. This was in 1992. I was in my own house, lying on a settee. It was about half-ten at night. I had twin boys and an older boy upstairs. Suddenly, my uncle appeared in front of me, with his glasses on him. He was the same healthy man he was before he got sick. He just looked at me and I could really see his face. I knew it was him. It all lasted about one minute.

The next thing, there was a big bang out in the hallway. It was like a whole dresser full of delft fell. I ran out, but nothing had fallen in the hall. I then ran upstairs, but my children were alright and nothing had fallen there either. I came back downstairs. The next morning, at ten o'clock, my two sisters arrived and told me that my uncle had died. He had died around the time he appeared to me. I didn't feel as bad about that as I felt around the death of my sister's baby. That was the worst one that happened and it was very hard on me.

All these experiences are very difficult to explain. I don't know what to think about them. I never speak to people about them or discuss them. I have been told that younger people tend to talk about them, but people tend to remain quieter as they get older because others wouldn't believe them. I always felt I would have liked to tell a priest or a minister, but I didn't. I just kept quiet and kept them to myself. All I know is that they happen at the time of a death or before a death. That's all I know.

JOHN, FROM COUNTY CORK, recollects a puzzling type of deathbed phenomenon experienced by both himself and his mother.

My mother had a brother, William, who was in the First World War. I think he had left school when he was about 14. His father was a mason and quite possibly he went into that trade as a very young lad. He eventually decided to join the British Army and he ended up based in France with the First Battalion of the Irish Guards. They were very rough times and a lot of violent battles were fought there. Things were very bad.

He was killed in September 1918, right at the end of the war, at the Canal du Nord, which is a big canal in northern France. He was only 18 when he died. He had been involved in the Allied offensive against the German Army that would eventually bring the war to a close. His body wasn't brought back to Ireland; instead, they buried him where he fell. The war ended two months later.

William was my mother's favourite brother. They had been exceptionally close. She was only 16 when he died, two years younger than him. They had grown up together in Wexford town. My mother eventually left the town after she met my father, who was from Glengarriff in County Cork. He was in the Irish Army and they eventually settled in Fermoy.

It was in Fermoy that my mother once told me how one Monday night, back in September 1918, while her brother was fighting in France, she saw a strange thing on the wall of the house where she was living. It looked like a Catherine wheel, which is a firework that goes around in a circle. She said it was like a star and was turning around and around. She was on her own at the time it took place. She said she knew immediately that William had died.

It was a shocking thing to happen. She was staggered and she told her family. Twelve days later, news came through informing the family of William's death. It transpired that he had died on the same Monday night in September 1918 that she had spotted the Catherine wheel on the wall. She had known on that previous Monday night that he was gone.

She informed me about what had happened when I was a schoolboy, about 14 years old. It was the only time she said it to me. She described it perfectly, although I never went into the full details with her, probably because I didn't really believe her. I thought she might have been romancing, that she was only imagining it or that she was daft.

That view of mine only lasted until I experienced the very same thing many years later. This was in the 1970s, when I was in my mid-30s. I was living in a block of flats in London. I was married, with a family, and I was working in the building trade. The flat I lived in was off the main road, with two windows, and it needed heavy curtains to keep out the sound of traffic.

One Monday night, I was asleep and my wife was asleep beside me in the bed. It was pitch-dark, around 12 o'clock. I suddenly woke up and I could see this Catherine wheel on the wall. It was like a flashing light, going around in a circle. It was spinning on the wall, up towards the top of the room, right beside the bed. It was just under the ceiling and it was coloured red and yellow. It was probably about eight inches in circumference and the whole thing lasted maybe 12 or 15 seconds.

I then heard someone or something saying, 'Your Aunt Mary is dead!' It just came into my head, into my mind. I didn't even know I had an Aunt Mary. I said to my wife, 'What did you say to me?' She just said, 'Go back to sleep, you're dreaming.' I sat there for a while wondering what this was all about and who this Aunt Mary was. It also struck me that this was like what my mother had seen all those years before.

I was stunned by what I had seen and I couldn't believe it. However, the following day, I decided to go back to work and I forgot about it. I thought that maybe my wife was right and that I was dreaming. That all changed, however, on the following Saturday when I went to visit my brother, who lived in Ladbroke Grove in London. I went because I was told that my mother and father had come over from Ireland to stay with him.

While I was there, my mother happened to say, 'By the way, your Aunt Mary died on Monday night!' It turned out that I had an Aunt Mary who was living in England and my parents had come across for the funeral. She was on my father's side of the family, but I didn't even know her. Not only had she died, but she had died on that same Monday night I had seen the Catherine wheel.

Although I know what happened was genuine, it has never occurred since then, which I find very strange. I have lost four members of my family in subsequent years: three brothers with cancer and a sister with a brain haemorrhage at the age of 35. My mother also died when she was 79. Yet I never experienced it again.

It does, though, make me feel that this thing runs in the family. I think when anyone in the family dies, someone else in the family gets a warning. I can't explain it, but I think that the warning definitely comes, yet I don't know why. It's just one of those strange things.

It also reinforces my belief in life after death. My personal experience, and my mother's experience, makes me convinced about that. I am a deeply religious person and I believe there is somewhere we go to up there. I also expect to meet my family again. It's like a caterpillar changes into a butterfly. We will change, too, and I look forward to it.

SINÉAD, FROM COUNTY TIPPERARY, had a peculiar visitation from her father around the time of his death.

It all dates back to a Friday in 2002. I was in my 30s at the time. It was just an ordinary day. My father had collected his shopping down the town and had brought a neighbour's granddaughters up to the railway station. That night, there were four of us in the house. My parents were watching *The Late Late Show*. I remember The Wolfe Tones were on. I went to bed a bit early. My brother went up to his room, too, probably watching his own TV. It really was just an ordinary night at the end of an ordinary day.

At about four o'clock in the morning, I woke up suddenly

out of my sleep. I had been dreaming that I was a little girl again and my father was going out the door to work. It was daylight. He was wearing the green overcoat that he wore at work at the time. I saw myself with blonde hair and curls. My father was saying goodbye to me.

As I woke up out of the dream, I had an awful pain in my chest. I also felt something up against my nose and when I looked I felt I could see a sheep. It was as if the sheep was rubbing his nose up against me to get my attention. I turned in the bed and I thought I could see the Good Shepherd. I then looked up and I felt I saw Jesus and he was holding a lamb in his arms and sheep were all around him. He had long auburn hair and lovely blue eyes.

It all felt really strange. It was almost like I was in shock. I wondered what was going on. I wondered was I dreaming. I also wondered, with the pain I was getting, if I was sick with some sort of bug or something. Yet it was all so real and I felt I could really see Jesus. I thought it was wonderful, although I worried that I was going to die. I asked myself, 'Has Jesus arrived to take me?' The whole thing probably lasted for about a minute; it's hard to know.

I decided to get up and I went downstairs. The next thing, my father came up the stairs towards me. I hadn't known he was up. I said, 'Are you alright?' He said, 'I'm fine!' I also asked him, 'Have you any pain?' Again, he said, 'I'm fine!' I don't know why I asked him if he had any pain, as there was no reason to do so. I was looking at him and his eyes were very blue. I looked at him and he looked at me for a minute or two.

Suddenly, I realised I could see through his chest. I could see his heart and everything. I felt his deep love for me and I expressed my profound love for him. Although it was all very strange, my father seemed real as could be and I was definitely awake. I then carried on to the bottom of the stairs, where I saw our collie dog. I said to him, 'Brandy, you won't be going out yet because it is too early in the morning.' After that, I decided, 'I'll go back up to bed again.'

I went into the bed and soon fell asleep. I was probably only asleep for a minute or so when I heard my mother calling my brother and me. She said, 'Come down, there's something wrong with your father!' My mother had apparently gone downstairs because my father was absent for a while and she wondered was he OK. She saw him lying flat out on the sitting-room floor and she lifted up his arm and it flopped down again.

I got some shock. My father was lying there with a lovely, peaceful face. We took his pulse and he was gone. It turned out that he had a massive heart attack. What he was doing downstairs, God only knows. He might have been going to the toilet or making a cup of tea, although this was around four o'clock in the morning.

It struck me that during that time when I was having the dream and the vision, he was obviously downstairs, probably dead. So what was my dream all about? What was the vision regarding Jesus and the Good Shepherd about? What had I seen on the stairs? Was my father dead or alive at the time? Was it some sort of spirit of him after he died? Why did it only happen to me? Why was he showing that he loved me?

I often think about it and I believe it must have been a vision of him that I saw on the stairs. I think he was saying goodbye to me. He must have been dead at the time and I wonder was it his spirit leaving his body. Maybe his spirit was returning upstairs to say goodbye to all of us, although the others saw nothing. I also wonder if the pain that I felt as

I woke up was me feeling his pain as he was having his heart attack.

What happened that night will stay with me for the rest of my life. It has made a big impact on me and given me great comfort. It has also told me something about death. It has made me believe there is something beyond. I think there is another world we will go to, much better than this.

I think those who have gone ahead of us are waiting for us there. I also believe I will meet my father again in heaven. I think Jesus is waiting for us, too, and I believe he'll come back for us. At the end of the day, I really don't know what happened that night or what was going on. But, somehow, I am convinced that my father came back to see me and to say goodbye.

BERNARD, FROM COUNTY MAYO, talks about his mother's visions regarding other people's deaths.

The first vision happened back in 1971. It took place in the month of May. I remember my brother and I had gone to a fair. We went in a Ford Cortina, which we were just after buying. My mother was at home and having her usual afternoon nap in her chair by the fire. It was probably one of those chilly May days where you still need a fire.

Suddenly, she had a vision. It involved her brother, who lived over in Manchester. She saw him coming up a bog road beside our house. It's a very old bog road that hasn't been maintained for years. She saw him at a particular corner on the road, at the beginning of one of our fields.

He wore a dark suit and he also carried a medium-brown suitcase. She knew there was something going to happen. Later that night, my grandmother took ill. I remember, when we returned home from the fair, our mother informed us that

Grandmother wasn't well. She was 88 years old and I think it was just old age was the problem. She passed away a week later.

Strangely, what my mother had seen in the vision came to pass around the time of the funeral. My uncle arrived back from Manchester in the same dark suit and with the same medium-brown suitcase. That's exactly what she had seen in the vision.

Eleven years later, in 1982, my mother had another vision. It was in late June. My mother told us that she had seen a red-haired woman coming in the front door. She was puzzled by what she saw and it didn't click with her. But when she thought about it, she realised it was my father's mother. She again knew something was going to happen.

The following day, my father got a heart attack. He had awful pains in his chest. He went into the hospital. There was a World Cup on at the time. I remember going into the hospital to see Dad and he was in the Intensive Care Unit. We went in there again, another day, and he was watching one of the World Cup matches. We were all excited that he was out of Intensive Care and doing well.

We all went in to see him yet another time and he said, 'There's no need to rush in tomorrow during the day. Leave it until the evening.' We travelled in that evening and we went to the ward, but he wasn't there. A doctor and nurse came out and asked to speak to my mother.

They brought us down another corridor. Just as they did so, my mother turned around and looked back. I don't know what prompted her to do that. She saw the porters running with a bed. It was my father in the bed. He was after getting a bad turn and he was dead.

A further strange thing happened when my mother died.

There's a woman who has prayer meetings and who lives not too far from us. My mother wasn't feeling well at the time. In fact, during Christmas 1989, she had said to all of us once Christmas dinner was over, 'This is the last Christmas I'll be with you!' In mid-January, she got sick and I brought her to the doctor. I also decided to bring her up to this woman's prayer meeting.

When the woman was saying the Rosary at the meeting, she suddenly stopped. She said, 'I see a boy and a girl sitting by a fire and they are crying.' She described the girl, who was my sister. On the way home, my mother said, 'That woman is cracked!' I think she had immediately recognised what the woman was talking about. It was her funeral! She died four weeks later.

I believe you would have to call what my mother saw 'visions'. She could foretell what was coming up. She wasn't an overly-religious woman by any standards. She would make sure we said our prayers before bed when we were young. We always went to Mass. But it wasn't a religious thing. She just had this ability to see things and they always surrounded death.

Nothing good was ever seen by my mother right up to the time she died in February 1990. Everything was bad and involved a pending departure. She never worried about them and she would tell us about them, as she did with the visions involving my grandmother and father. They never worried any of us in the family. They were just part of life and part of the way we were.

There's another strange thing about the deaths though. My grandfather died in 1961, my grandmother died in 1971, my dad died in 1982 and my mother died in 1990. In the year 2000, I had a cousin, a priest, who died. They all died at the very beginning of each new decade. So when it comes to the end of a decade, we're all looking at one another asking, 'Who's going to be next?'

PAT, FROM COUNTY DONEGAL, recalls some strange events that occurred over half a century ago.

A couple of incidents happened when I was only a child. I was brought up for much of the time in my grandparents' house in Donegal. It was a very close-knit community, with reasonably-sized farms and very small businesses. We're talking about the 1950s and 1960s.

There was a local man there who had retired from the army, where he had been an officer or a quartermaster or something similar. He regularly walked up and down the road, going to the shop and collecting his pension and things like that. Every time he passed, he would come into my granny's house and she made tea for him. We all knew him quite well.

This ex-army man had something that was very rare in the area – a brand-new bicycle. Nobody had brand-new bicycles. Even when you got a 'new' one, it was second-hand. To see a new one was a novelty, but he had one. It stood out.

One Sunday morning, we were all going to our local 11 o'clock Mass. We were waiting for my uncle, who drove a car. He probably had been out the night before and was a bit slow to get up in the morning. We were dressed and ready to go and waiting for this man to drive us.

My grandmother's house was high up, with a hill at the bottom of the yard which was very steep. It sloped down to the main road. I was standing on the slope, looking down towards the road, when I saw this ex-army man with his brand-new bicycle walking up against the hill.

When I looked around, I saw my grandmother standing behind me. I hadn't known she was there. She just put her hand on my shoulder. Neither of us said anything. We then got ready to travel to Mass. When we got into the chapel, just before the Mass began, the priest announced that this same man had been found dead early that morning, at about seven o'clock or so.

I never really found out what had happened to him. I was only around ten years of age – 13 at most – at that time and too young to know the details. However, I do know how he was found. Two girls were on their way to early Mass in the town, which was at 7.30 in the morning. They were cycling about a mile or a mile-and-a-half from the town when they saw a walking-stick in a hedge.

They looked in through the hedge and the man was lying flat on his back on the green grass, with nothing disturbed. His coat and belt were tied. He was just lying there, with his hands by his side. There was nothing violent about his death. I think he must have had a heart attack. That had obviously happened a long time before I saw him with his bicycle down below my grandmother's house.

When we were on the way back from the Mass, my grandmother told everybody what she had seen. I think she spoke about it when we were returning in my uncle's car. She mentioned that she had seen the man with his bicycle just before 11 o'clock Mass. She said something like, 'The poor man. I could have sworn I saw him this morning.' It was said like that.

She put it in such a way that if you believed in that sort of thing then you would accept it, but if you didn't believe you could just pass it off. That was the way people spoke; they didn't make any definitive statements. Although she wasn't surprised by it, she didn't force her views on anyone else.

She also asked me, 'Did you see him, too?' I said, 'I think I did.' She maintained that she couldn't see him until she had put her hand on my shoulder. Nobody remarked on what she said. That also was the way it was; the observation would be left there in mid-air and people would remember it even if they never commented on it again.

My grandmother certainly believed it had happened and she was definite in her own mind. She just took it that it was a visit from an old friend. He was a good friend of hers and the way she explained it to me was, 'He just came to visit me. That was his last visit.' What she meant was that it was a last visit made around the time he died.

There was another event, which happened with my father. There was a house directly across the road from us, up a little hill. You could see it plainly from our house as it was little more than 50 yards from door to door. My father was very friendly with the family who lived there, especially the man of the house. They were best friends.

One Sunday morning, my father was at home on his own and boiling potatoes. The rest of us were at Mass. He was straining water off the potatoes, by the drain at the back door. He looked over to the other house and he saw what he thought was his friend. He was dressed in those overalls that men used to wear years ago, which was a normal dress for him. It was so like him that my father believed he had seen him.

It turned out later that the man had been at Mass at the time. My father learned that information when he went over to the house in the afternoon. He actually went over to discuss what he saw. He must have been concerned. His friend was extremely worried, too, and he thought he was going to die. They both took it very seriously.

A few days later, a letter or a telegram or some other kind of communication arrived from America pointing out that his friend's cousin had died there. My father immediately believed that he hadn't seen his friend that morning; instead, he saw the cousin. He believed it was a message that he was given to pass on. He thought the explanation behind what happened was that if his friend had got the message himself he would become alarmed, but because it was transmitted through my father the blow would be softened.

Regarding the death of the ex-army man with the bicycle, I have always believed that I saw this incident happen. I'd say I believed it up to ten years ago. In recent years, however, I don't believe that I did. I have reviewed the whole thing and I have come to the conclusion that I mustn't have seen it at all, although I might be wrong.

What happened is hard to explain. Whatever about seeing the man, I have problems with the bicycle. The bicycle kept niggling at me. I just cannot believe I saw it. How can you account for the image of a person plus bicycle? Bicycles don't have souls!

It's not that I disbelieve all events like this. For example, there was another thing that took place when I was even younger. My grandfather was in the hospital and we were living in a house nearby. I was with my mother. We were walking down towards my grandfather's house and we saw him up ahead of us. I remember my mother saying, 'There's Granddad, he must have got out of hospital.'

When we got down to his house, however, he wasn't there at all. He was still in the hospital. That one I am prepared to believe because all you had was the image of a person. But how can you account for a bicycle?

I have thought about the man with the bicycle a lot and I feel there must have been something else at work, maybe not an optical illusion but a mental illusion. My mind must have been confused. I suppose, over the years, my faith has also deteriorated and I have come to the point where I don't believe there is anything after death.

Throughout Donegal, however, a lot of beliefs like these still live on. A man once said to me, 'Donegal is like Switzerland; it's completely surrounded by mountains.' It's a county where the language and tradition have survived. Life in Donegal in the 1930s was similar to what it had been 100 or 200 years previously. It hadn't changed and the modern world hadn't intruded at that stage.

People didn't disregard events like the ones I have just described. When they got a message or a sign that somebody was about to die, they took it seriously. They were so serious about these signs that if they concerned somebody who was dying locally and the person was their responsibility, they would actually start preparing the house for the wake. That's how certain they were.

Whether the predicted events invariably came to pass is something that we don't know. But they were relied on in tradition, so they must have worked. If they didn't work on three or four occasions, they would be disregarded and wouldn't be believed anymore. The fact that they were still believed up into the twentieth century means they must have been reliable in the past.

Probably the first thing that brought the modern world to Donegal was electrification in the 1950s and '60s. However, today, especially among older people, these beliefs, including folklore about people appearing before their deaths, live on in the communal psyche or in the culture or whatever you might call it. And even if I now might not believe, my grandmother and father were sure that what they saw was real and they certainly believed in them.

KATHLEEN, FROM COUNTY KERRY, had an unusual experience about a week after her mother died. It happened in October 2010.

My mother lived in a bungalow across from the farm where we had all been reared. She had moved out to the bungalow following my father's death many years before. She was on her own there for 26 years. My brother lived just across from her in the old farmhouse and I lived just over the road. It meant that I met my mother a lot.

As my mother got older, I would take care of her and take her out every day. I'd bring her for a walk on the beach, out for the shopping and to the doctor. We got on very well. She was a nice woman and easy to get along with. She liked the bit of fun and she liked to sing a song. I think her favourite was 'She Moved Through the Fair'. She was a very popular woman.

In the last year of her life, she had a few chest infections and she went into hospital once or twice. In February 2010, she got very sick and had to be hospitalised. After she came home, she was alright, but she got sick once more and had to be hospitalised again. She then started complaining about her stomach.

She was waiting for a scan of her stomach, but it was put back and put back. It was September before she got it done. The scan showed an ulcer, which was cancerous. The doctor said that it might stay as it was for a while, because she was old, and she gave her some tablets to take. Unfortunately, my mother went down very fast.

I remember she had to go into hospital about three weeks later. We were waiting all the evening for her to get a bed. Unfortunately, she then got some kind of attack. After that, everything happened so quickly. She died at 11.30 on Sunday morning, 10 October 2010, aged 90. Afterwards, for a while, I stayed in the bungalow across from the farm and my sister, who had arrived back for the funeral, stayed there, too.

I remember one night, exactly four days after my mother was buried, my sister had gone to bed and I didn't feel like going to sleep. I started sorting out some bits and pieces. I found some bills and things from my mother's friends, all in a big handbag. I threw out what was of no use. I then went to bed. It was about 12.30 at night.

I was lying there when suddenly I woke up with a start. I was having a bad dream about some sort of war. It was probably around three o'clock in the morning. I felt afraid, so I sat up in bed hoping to get over it. I put on the light. I wasn't really a dreamer, although I would have one now and again. This night, however, stood out.

I was resting, half sitting up in bed and coming back to myself, when suddenly everything went very calm. Everything became very quiet. It was as if I was waiting for something. I think I was in a bit of a trance. I wasn't afraid in the least, even though I had turned the light off again, but it was a strange feeling.

Suddenly, I felt a huge surge of energy come into me from outside. It was like a big 'whoosh', almost like a bird had entered me. It felt like it was taking me over, going right to my core. The effect was almost like a whirlwind inside of me, like it came into my soul and it stayed there for a little while.

It was as though something supernatural had happened, but it is hard to describe.

I couldn't move. It felt like everything in me had stopped, including my blood. It wasn't that I felt paralysed, just that everything had come to a halt. That went on for maybe five minutes, but I don't really know; I wasn't watching the time. I just stayed there in the bed without moving.

The energy then left me, again like a bird. I could feel it going. It flew around the room. It was a bit like a balloon with the air going out of it. The noise from it sounded like that, like a 'whoosh'. The thing then went out through the curtain and out through the window. The window was a big one over to my left and the curtain was shut. From where I was, I could see a black spot on the curtain where it went out. I could see the spot even though there was little light in the room.

I then slowly came back to myself. I thought of calling my sister, but nothing would come out of my mouth. I had no voice and I couldn't form words. Strangely, I felt very calm. It was too early to get up, so I waited until six o'clock or seven o'clock and then I went in and told her. I'm sure she was half-asleep and she didn't say anything for a while.

Eventually, after I had returned back into my room, she followed me with her pillow. She talked about what I had said to her and she wanted to know all about what had happened. I said that I thought it had something to do with my mother saying goodbye to me. I especially thought that because it happened in her house. My sister thought it was something to do with my mother saying goodbye, too.

The following day, I told the parish priest, but he didn't say anything; instead, he just listened to me. My sister also told a next-door neighbour, who was a priest and a family friend, and he said that what happened was very special. He said it was a privilege that it had happened to me. I believe that, too. After that, I told the rest of my family, but I didn't say it to any more people. Instead, I kept it to myself.

I believe that what took place was something from the afterlife. It certainly wasn't like I was expecting it. And I hadn't gone to bed thinking it would happen. Instead, I think it was some sort of sign from my mother. I believe she was telling me, from wherever she had gone, that there is something more there, some sort of life after death. I think what happened had something to do with that.

I believe her soul either came back to me or maybe it hadn't departed yet. There's an old belief around here, which my mother-in-law used to bring up, 'The soul doesn't leave the body until around the fourth day.' Maybe, then, her soul was departing the house at the time it happened.

What occurred didn't make me any holier in the church sense, although I always go off to Mass on a Sunday and, whenever I think of them, I say some prayers. But I do believe the soul lives on and that there is something there, some sort of different life which we eventually pass on to. Whatever the truth might be, I know something happened that night in October 2010. It was something completely different and it has never happened before or since.

MARY, FROM COUNTY DUBLIN, lost her granddaughter to cancer in 2002. The evening before the child's death, she had a vision predicting what was about to happen.

My daughter's child, Emily, was born in 1996. She was a beautiful baby. I remember going up to see her in the maternity hospital when she was born. She had beautiful eyes; I'll always remember that. I looked after her for about five-and-a-half months because my daughter had postnatal depression. I did everything for her and I bought her lots of things. I wheeled her around the country roads. I loved her dearly.

I then had a bit of bad luck with illness and had to go into hospital. It was a difficult time. We were told we would have to get someone to look after her at least temporarily. My daughter's friends had wanted to adopt her. They ended up fostering her and looking after her. I remember leaving the child into their arms. She was five-and-a-half months old at the time.

Emily grew up to be a beautiful child, very intelligent. She was very bright and a lovely singer. We saw her a lot. She always wanted to go shopping and we would bring her out. She always had beautiful clothes and she loved her mammy and she loved me. I know she was totally happy.

Unfortunately, she developed cancer when she was three years of age. She had been unwell for a while and was crying in pain. Initially, no one could find anything wrong with her. Eventually, she went to see a specialist and he found a little tumour in the soft tissue in the heel of her foot. It was diagnosed as a form of cancer called Ewing's sarcoma, which is very aggressive and very painful. She was brought in for treatment.

She loved it in the hospital, playing with the other children. She got treated with radiotherapy and chemotherapy. All her hair fell out. She then went into remission. She went to school and was very bright. She met Westlife and went to Lourdes and Euro Disney in Paris. Unfortunately, she was never cured and only had nine months in remission.

I remember when her cancer returned. She was amazingly brave. She came to the door and said, 'My cancer is back. I'll tell my mammy myself. Am I going to die?' They left her out of the hospital after deciding that she should have her last months in her own place, with people she was used to. She lost the use of her legs and had to use a chair. It was a very sad time.

The children in her Montessori school said to her at the beginning of the holidays, 'Bye, bye. We will see you next September.' Her answer was, 'Oh, no! You won't see me in September. I'm going to be an angel.' Later, the priest came down and he blessed her and said, 'If everybody had as little baggage as that child, they'd be alright and go to heaven.'

The day before she died, I was down in my back room. It's cool down there and I could hear the birds outside. I was in bed and praying to St. Anthony, St. Joseph and St. Padre Pio, who are three of my favourite saints. I had always prayed to them, asking them to help Emily. The room was dark. It was about five o'clock or half-five in late summer. I was in a lot of pain, crying and asking for Emily to be left with us.

All of a sudden, I saw this man in front of my eyes. He looked so real. It was St. Joseph, exactly as I had seen him in a statue in a church. He wore a sort of long, brown tweed coat. His face looked beautiful, full of compassion. I never saw a face like it in my life. There was a baby in his arms, with a little wrap around its tummy. It was a younger child than Emily and I could see the bare feet.

He never said anything, not a word. He just looked at me compassionately. He had the child up near his beard. It was as if he was showing me the baby. He then disappeared. The whole thing didn't last long. It's hard to put a time on it; it was more like a 'flash'. I said, 'Thank you, St. Joseph.' I knew it was a sign and a message. I felt he had come to me before Emily died to tell me what was about to happen. I knew that he wasn't going to leave her with me; instead, he was taking her to heaven.

The next day, we got a call to say Emily wasn't well. We went over to see her and she was very, very ill. She was lying on a sofa. At 7.20 in the evening, she passed away. I was with her, saying a Hail Mary. She went without a word. She died on 3 August 2002, with me holding her hand. She was three weeks away from her sixth birthday when she died.

We were all heartbroken. She had been such a very special person, even though she was only here for such a short time. The pain was overwhelming. I cried all the time. I also know her mother wasn't very happy that God had taken her to heaven. But we all knew that God had loved her and God was minding her and God had made her. It's just that God wanted her back. She had gone through a lot of pain and it was a happy release.

Looking back, I believe St. Joseph came and told me that Emily was going to heaven. He was telling me that she was going to peace and happiness. He knew the pain I was in as a grandmother. He was the foster-father of Jesus Christ and I believe he understood how much I was suffering. I believe he came to me to put me out of my misery.

I still have everything to do with Emily exactly as it was before she left. I have her little table, all her clothes and all of her toys. I used to bathe her as a baby at the table. Her clothes still smell of her. I have dreamt of her, too, smiling and waving at me. It means that she is happy. I would prefer her to be with us, but it just wasn't to be. She is in a beautiful place. And I believe she is looking after all the little angels in heaven, where we will all meet again.

VINNY, FROM COUNTY GALWAY, who we heard from earlier in this book, describes a strange event from the late 1980s.

A close family friend, my godfather actually, was coming home from America and we were down collecting him at Shannon Airport. He had been visiting family there. His flight was due to arrive at around 11 o'clock or 11.30 at night. My mother, sister and I were in the car, which was a green Mazda 323 hatchback. I was only about five years of age, my sister was in her early teens and my mother was doing the driving.

Unfortunately, we got the date wrong. We were a day early and we had to return home empty-handed. We were coming back to Galway, up through County Clare, on small country roads. I remember it vividly. I was sitting in the middle of the car, in the back, with my hands on each of the two seats in the front. My sister was in the front passenger seat, on my left. My mother was driving, sitting to my right. I didn't want to miss anything.

I remember it was very late at night and we were passing through a bog. There were no fences or hedges on the sides of the road. It was pitch-dark, sometime around late October. It was the middle of the night, coming up to four o'clock, not dawn yet. The car was quiet and we were just driving along.

All of a sudden, without any warning, my mother stopped the car. She turned off the engine, got out and walked up the road. I turned to my sister to ask for an explanation. She had no idea and was wondering herself what was going on. I got out of the car and I ran up to my mother, who was now a good bit up the road. I started tugging at her and asking, 'What's going on? What's going on?' My sister came up as well.

She turned around to me and she put her finger to her lip as if to say, 'Sshh!' She then pointed up with her index finger and said, 'Look up!' I did and above me was this incredible light, which just sat there in the sky. It was like as if the sky had unzipped and opened up and revealed this light. The light was the whitest of white, although it wasn't glaring or blinding like the sun would be. Everything was completely dark around it.

The light was huge, about the size of ten football fields. Its breadth was about half its length. It just sat there over us and was very visible. It was like as if it had opened up just for us. It wasn't that we were near any town, so that can't explain it. Nor was the dawn breaking. I had never seen anything like it and I can still see it in my mind.

Mammy had started to cry. The tears were falling down her face. As she looked up, she said, 'That's the angels going for Carmel!' Carmel was a relation of the family who, at the time, was dying of cancer. It was a severe form of cancer and she had it for a good number of years. Mammy just knew that Carmel had died. As I was looking up, all I remember thinking was, 'Heaven!' I think I said, 'That's lovely.'

The light stayed there for about three minutes and then it closed in on itself and shot up the country, heading northeast. The light started dwindling, getting smaller and smaller. It disappeared from in front of us. It was moving in the direction of where Carmel lived. It was gone before we knew it and everything went dark again. It was the strangest thing; it was there and it was gone, lasting three minutes, in the middle of nowhere.

What happened didn't faze me, as I was a child. I suppose I felt, 'If Mammy says that, it must be true.' We then went to the car. Mammy looked at the clock to see the time. I remember it was ten-to-four. We then headed off home.

We arrived back home at around the half-seven mark in the

morning. Dad met us at the door. He had obviously heard the car coming in the gate and was waiting for us. I remember his facial expression. Mam just looked at him. The first thing he said to us was, 'Carmel died this morning at ten-to-four!' I remember thinking, 'God! Mam was right!' To me, it was proof.

After that, we became involved in the funeral and all of the action surrounding it and we simply forgot about what had happened. However, Mam did describe it to the sisters of the lady who had died. They were actually very pleased to hear it. I remember they blessed themselves and said, 'Thank God!'

Otherwise, my family and I never really discussed it since. I did raise it once with my sister and she had no explanation. She studied science and I know if there was any explanation she would have come up with it. I also once spoke about it with my mother. She just got a bit emotional over Carmel and said, 'What happened was a real blessing. It was lovely that God showed it to us.' But she didn't dwell on it much.

It's very hard to think of an explanation. Mam couldn't have simply guessed at Carmel's death by chance. I mean, Carmel had cancer that lasted around five years; it wasn't just something that lasted six weeks. She had gone to Mass on the Sunday previous to it. So it couldn't have been just guesswork by my mother or that she hit on the death by chance. Instead, my mother was under no illusion as to what was happening.

It also left a big impression on me, partly because I was so young and didn't question what happened. I just noted it for what it was. I think I saw the truth of it straight away. I felt God had shown us that he'd taken Carmel away. Within the next six years, I discovered prayer and my faith strengthened. It helped open up my faith.

I can still see what happened to this day. I remember the road, the bog, the colour of the night. I remember the colour of the light, the size of it, the colour of the car, where I was sitting, even down to the shoes I was wearing, every detail. It was huge and it will stay with me for the rest of my life.

MARGARET, FROM COUNTY LONGFORD, remembers how her parish priest saw an apparition of someone who was dying.

I used to look after a parish priest, who was a relation. He was an intensely spiritual person and a man of great faith. Compassion and kindness were two of his attributes. He was a wonderful writer. He was also a great friend and a lovely man. He really was. But he wasn't a tough guy; he needed a bit of minding.

He lived very close by, about two miles away, in the parish house. It was a modern bungalow. I used to prepare the dinner, which we would call lunch nowadays. I also tidied up. In the evening, he used to sit in the sitting-room at the back, which was a very simple room with a three-piece suite and a fire to the right. There was a window the length of the wall at the back. It looked out on the garden.

We had a bit of a routine in the evenings. He would read his office and I would then go in to him with coffee and some biscuits. I remember one night, when it was dark, I went in to him as usual with the coffee around eight o'clock. He was sitting in his chair facing the window, reading the office.

Suddenly, he said to me, 'There's somebody after dying in the parish!' I said, 'I never heard the phone.' I thought he must have got a phone call and I was puzzled because I never heard it ring. He said, 'It's not that. It's just that somebody has passed the back window. He was wearing a check jacket. I'm going to pray for that person now.'

He didn't seem in the least bit shocked. I gave him the coffee and I went out. He started praying and didn't have the coffee. Just then, the phone rang. Somebody was looking for the priest. After he came off the phone, he said to me, 'There's been an accident!' He ran out, while I waited.

After he arrived back, he told me that a neighbour of ours, who we knew, had been killed. He was an older man, who was a very nice, wholesome and decent person. He was killed riding his bicycle at the crossroads. He was wearing a check jacket. He always wore the same check jacket, like the sort of one you would wear to the races. I said, 'My goodness! Was that him passing the window, do you think?'

He said, 'He probably needed prayer and I prayed for him. He was obviously dying at the time.' He had no doubt whatsoever about what had happened. A lot of other priests mightn't have taken it seriously, but he did. He was that type of person. He was a very stable, solid man.

I have never forgotten it. I believe God granted the man who died the prayer he needed. I think he was allowed to call to the house, seeking prayer. He was obviously sent to the right man because the request was taken very seriously and prayers were said. I really believe that. It has also helped me believe that there's more to life than we know.

I often hear people talk about how dead people appear to them and sometimes I don't believe what they say. I don't think that life after death is all about wandering back here again. I believe God has a place for us and a job for us. I believe we have to do the job as best we can while we are here and then he will recompense us when we go to him. In this case, however, I also believe that what happened was definitely real.

Regarding the priest, he was diagnosed with cancer on 28 February 1995. He was in hospital in Dublin for three weeks and I went up to see him every day. One morning, he rang and he said, 'You're coming up today?' I said, 'Yeah, I'm coming up.' He said, 'Do come, because I have cancer on both lungs.' He wasn't even a smoker. I went up and he got in the car and came home with me. I took care of him for three months and he died on 4 June 1995.

The week before he died, he said to me, 'I have asked God for a favour.' I said, 'Have you?' I thought maybe he had asked that he would be cured. He said, 'I asked God that you would be the only one with me when I go.' I didn't really want to talk to him about what he had said, because I didn't want him to think about dying. But what he said did make me think that when there were people around, he wouldn't die. The more people that came, the better I felt. I was playing tricks in my mind. But I left it and didn't say anything.

Eventually, one Sunday, there were lots of people around. His brother was there. There also was an ordination in the diocese and because the priests knew he was ill, they came and visited. That day, the bishop, 22 priests and I don't know how many other people came to visit our house. Our garden was full of people. Everybody was filing in and out and talking to him and blessing him and saying a prayer with him. I thought, 'He won't die because there are so many people here.'

I stayed outside for a few minutes with my son. After a while, he said, 'Go in, you're needed.' So I walked into the house. I then walked into the bedroom. As I did so, it was like as if everybody left. Nobody was there, but me and him.

I can still see his hand coming up from under the sheet. He reached out and he took my hand and looked straight at me. And he died! There was nobody there, but the two of us. His wish had come true.

SINÉAD, FROM COUNTY GALWAY, outlines what her grandmother witnessed when her great-grandmother was dying in Dublin.

My grandmother was born in the 1920s and she came from County Galway. She often described to me how her mother, my great-grandmother, was dying in hospital in Dublin. Her mother was quite young, but had been ill for a long time. I think she was in her 50s or 60s. It might have been cancer; I'm not sure. Whatever it was, it was very serious, which was why she was in Dublin.

One day, the family travelled to Dublin and they were all waiting outside of my great-grandmother's bedroom in the hospital, in the waiting area. Suddenly, my grandmother saw a man walking into the room. No one else saw him, only her. Although he just looked like an ordinary man, she said she immediately knew it was St. Michael, the Archangel.

She said she had seen him before, at other points in her life. It wasn't only when people were dying, but on other occasions. She especially saw him when she was younger. She later said that she hadn't seen him since that time with her mother in hospital. But on that day, in Dublin, she couldn't take her eyes off the door and he never came out.

She started freaking out and she got really upset. She said to her father and to whoever else was there, 'That was St. Michael! He's come to take my mother! She's gone!' Her father was really annoyed and said, 'Would you stop saying things like that.' But they were all sufficiently worried to go into the room and there was nobody there. There was no man in there. They also discovered, however, that her mother had passed away. She was dead.

My grandmother has often said that, once her own time comes, she will see St. Michael again. It's not necessarily that she would be scared when it happens, but she sees him as a bad omen. She has also said that since her mother died, she would appear to her in dreams. She said that whenever it occurs, something terrible happens. Somebody becomes ill or dies.

She has told almost everyone the story of what happened in Dublin. She has told it the same way every time. She remembers it exactly as it took place. The wording is always the same. She is certainly not senile, far from it. I believe that she saw what she said she saw. I wouldn't question her. She has always firmly believed it, too.

KATHLEEN, FROM COUNTY KERRY, reveals that her brother appeared to her in dreams around the time of his death.

My brother was quite young, in his 50s, and he was dying. He had a series of strokes. We had been called to his deathbed a number of times. You couldn't even sense life in him towards the end. He was totally disabled at this stage. All his functions had stopped and he wasn't able to walk. It was as if he was gone already. As a family, we stayed with him and said the Rosary and things like that.

On one occasion, the doctor said that he wouldn't survive the night. We were instructed to say our goodbyes. We were also told to decide who would stay with him for the night; there was no point in us all staying. The doctor guaranteed us that he wouldn't be alive in the morning.

We decided who would stay at the hospital. I agreed with the person who stayed that she would ring me at six o'clock the following morning and I would collect her. We said our goodbyes and I went home. The others went home, too. It took me a while to get to sleep, but I succeeded eventually.

In the morning, the telephone rang at six o'clock. I went down and answered it. I was told, 'You won't believe it. He is still alive.' I said, 'My goodness! Are you serious?' I was really surprised. We decided that there was no need for me to go in and collect the person who had stayed overnight, so I went back to sleep after a while.

The minute I fell asleep, my brother appeared to me in a dream. He was kneeling down and his hands were held up in prayer. He was clearly before me. He said nothing, but his hands were joined in a pleading manner. In reality, because of his strokes, he couldn't kneel, but he could as he appeared to me. This lasted for a while and then he vanished.

When I woke up later, I said, 'He's not ready to go yet.' I felt there was something not quite done. The fact that he knelt before me and was pleading as if in prayer made me feel that. When I got up, I didn't tell anyone, but I went and I got Masses said for him. It took another week, until the following Sunday morning, for him to die. That was exactly a week after he appeared to me.

Not long after he died, he came to me again in a dream. In this dream, he was a young man and he had all his faculties. He was aged between 25 and 30. He was running. There was a crowd after him and he wasn't alone. He was happy, full of life and full of joy. He looked fresh and well.

When I woke up the following morning, I felt I had been somewhere else. I felt he had been trying to draw me across to another dimension, to heaven. I somehow felt I had been there for a short time, but I wasn't ready to go there permanently yet. I was very happy because I knew that he was happy, too, and I knew that everything was fine. I knew he had passed over.

I don't think these are just ordinary dreams. I have dreams all the time, but I knew these were different. These were not like those stupid dreams about things that happen during the day and that don't make sense. You forget them immediately. These dreams have a real meaning. They stand out and you never forget them. They are more like visions and they carry a very definite message.

Dreams like these feature very prominently in the Bible. For example, when St. Joseph was going to leave Mary after he discovered she was pregnant, he didn't know what to do or how he would do it. At night, he had a dream where an angel came to him and said that he wasn't to be afraid to marry Mary and that she was to be the Mother of God.

There were plenty of other dreams in the Bible, too, like when the Three Wise Men were told to take a different route home after their visit to the baby Jesus because Herod was a threat to them. A third involved an angel appearing to St. Joseph telling him to take Mary and Jesus to Egypt because Herod was about to slaughter innocent children. Dreams certainly feature extensively in the Bible.

I really believe that in the first dream I had about my brother, he came to me because he needed something. In the second dream, he came back to tell me he was happy and that whatever had delayed him from going over had been resolved.

I think that we all commit sins and do things that are wrong. The sins have to be made up for through acts of charity or prayer or whatever. I figure that he had to make up for a number of things that he had done in his life and they weren't compensated for. I felt that the extra week and the Masses I got said paved the way for him to cross over to heaven.

ANGELA, FROM COUNTY MEATH, had visions of her soul mate not long after he died.

I met my soul mate in 2002. I know this sounds corny, but we were meant to be together. That really was the case. We were very close. If I wasn't with him, I knew exactly what he was doing, what he was thinking about and where he was. The connection was unbelievable. He mirrored me and I mirrored him. I learned about myself through him. I think you are very lucky if you get this even once in your lifetime.

Even though he was my soul mate, we split up in 2005. He could be hard work at times. Then, unfortunately, he died through misadventure in 2006. His body was found in a canal, but no one could establish what had happened. I can remember one of his sisters rang to say what had occurred. It was a big shock to me and I wasn't expecting it. I was devastated. I am over it now, but it took me a long time.

A couple of months after he died, I was asleep when a strange thing happened to me. It's hard to explain. It felt like my spirit had gone out of my body. I knew I was still in my body, but something had left it. It was like I was having an out-of-body experience and I felt very strange. It wasn't at all like a dream.

I travelled to a place where I could see a river. I was standing on the edge of it and looking over to the far side. There was no particular colour to the river; instead, it was just like a dark, grey mass. It was extremely still. Beyond the river was an area that was very desolate and there wasn't much taking place. There was just grass there, nothing else. Everything was very still and quiet.

My soul mate was on the other side and he was standing beside this house, which was to the right of him. It was like an old, grey, two-storey, derelict house. It was on a hill, which was sloping downwards. He didn't look particularly happy or unhappy. His expression was sort of neutral, but he was looking directly at me as if he had to convey a message.

He really looked the exact same as he was when he was alive. He had a waistcoat on, with a black pair of trousers and also a white shirt. His brown hair was tied back in a ponytail. There was a running joke we had when we were together, where he would say, 'You'll never catch me wearing a suit.' He really wasn't into wearing suits at all. He wasn't wearing one that time either.

He had a rose in his hand and he was saying to me, 'I'll be waiting for you on the other side when it's your turn to go.' That's all he communicated to me. I know now why he said that. It was because he knew I was devastated by his death. He knew I felt it would be the end of us. He had come to console me because he knew I missed him.

I felt ecstatic the following day. I found it very difficult to understand what had happened, but I was so happy. I knew it wasn't the end, but that I would see him again. And when I thought about it, I felt I had been on the edge of the other side. It was definitely only the edge as I couldn't cross the river. That was because, as he said, it wasn't my time.

I had other visions of him, too. One happened at a stage when I was neither awake nor asleep. I was almost asleep, but not quite. I could observe him in my mind's eye walking across from the right-hand side to the left-hand side at the bottom of my bed. It was like he was just walking on through, like he was checking in on me to see if I was OK.

He had the same clothes on which he wore when he was

alive, including a navy sweatshirt with light-blue sleeves and blue denim jeans. I was amazed. It felt great that he hadn't forgotten me, but he was still with me. He was around and watching over me. It happened just before I was due to get up and I was very pleased.

I had another vision, where he was in this hospital. It was a long, grey building, with long corridors, like something you would see in Victorian times. It was very old-fashioned, with high ceilings. It was horrible. I was with him, although I wasn't supposed to be there. He was trying to say to me that he was recuperating until he healed and got better. He was telling me to go because I wasn't supposed to be there. I know I didn't stay long.

There was a further occasion when I was with him. There was this elevated embankment, which was all coloured green. Everything was green; there were no flowers. It was quiet and still. There wasn't a sound to be heard. You could hear a pin drop. He was over to the right of me. He was walking, but I was happy to sit there by myself, surrounded by nature. It was relaxing. He was around me, but he was doing his own thing.

Looking back, I know if I was to tell people about these happenings, they would think I was bonkers. But they were very real. I couldn't imagine or invent those things if I tried. I thought about them a lot after they took place and I believe that what I saw was what was happening on the other side. They have helped me believe in an afterlife.

At one stage, I used to dread dying, but now I don't. I wouldn't want a slow, difficult death, but the actual fear of dying is gone. That's because I know my soul mate will be waiting for me when it's my time to go. I know he was the one I was meant to be with in this life, but I also know he will be waiting for me when I die. We will be together again.

That's very reassuring to me, and I think it will be a happy place for both of us to be.

LOUIS, FROM COUNTY KILDARE, had a disturbing experience of a deceased person while in the course of his work.

I was a cleaner and a fitter of carpets and was working in a house about 40 years ago in Dublin. It was a red-brick, semi-detached property on the main Ranelagh Road, a pre-1930s house with big bay windows. There were three bedrooms and I was upstairs. It was in summertime, around July. I was doing a job there on my own. I was told I was the only one in the house, while the couple, who were middle-aged, were at work.

I was upstairs in the bedroom working away. I was down on my knees, cleaning the carpets, over near the chimney-breast, with my back to the door. The place was silent and quiet. The next thing, I felt this presence beside me. It was a really strong feeling. I didn't hear any sound, but it felt as if somebody had walked into the room. I wasn't frightened, but I thought it was odd. It was around three o'clock in the afternoon and bright.

I turned around. When I did so, there was this man standing at the door. He was stopped there and was just looking at me, observing what I was doing. He was aged in his 60s or there-abouts, about six feet tall, a good bit bigger than me and with reddish hair. Although I can't remember what he was dressed in, I said something to him and I thought it was odd that he didn't answer me back. Instead, he gave me a big smile.

He then went into the bathroom at the back of the house and after that he returned to his bedroom, which was the box-room in the front. He didn't disappear or anything; he just walked away. I assumed he must have been sleeping in the box-room, got up, went to the toilet and just returned to bed. I thought nothing about it and put it out of my mind and got on with my work.

Around teatime, while it was still very bright, the couple arrived home from their places of work. When the woman of the house came in, she walked upstairs and asked me, 'How are you getting on? Are you going well? Would you like a cup of tea?' I said to her, 'I thought I was in the house on my own.' She said, 'So you are.' I said, 'There's been a man at the door, smiling and looking at what I was doing.' She said, 'What? What sort of man?' So I told her. I said, 'He was a tallish man, with reddish hair, who came to the door and went back into the bedroom.'

At that, she raced down the stairs in a terrible state. She said nothing to me. A few minutes later, the husband came up and asked me, 'What did you say again to my wife?' So I told him and he stated, 'That man you described was my wife's father and only two months ago he died in that bedroom he came out of!' Apparently, he had died in the box-room.

I'm sure the two of them must have been shocked. I was probably too young to be shocked at the time, although I was puzzled by what had happened. It's hard to explain it. I have thought about it a lot and I often wondered if it might be a case of souls not reaching their destination, who get lost somewhere in the cosmos. Maybe that's what I saw.

I believe our souls eventually go to somewhere, either to heaven or hell. You know the way we say, 'Thank God, he's not suffering any more, he's gone to heaven.' I'm not sure it's like that. I think there's a place where we stop over before we go to heaven. I think it's a resting-place, perhaps purgatory.

The souls there need to be put to rest and we can do it by praying for them. If we can get them to heaven, I believe they help us here on earth and bring us peace. I think I had a glimpse of someone from that resting-place that day. I will never forget it and can still see what happened as if it was yesterday.

MARY, FROM COUNTY DOWN, recalls how angels protected her around the time she was undergoing a major surgical procedure.

I had open-heart surgery some years ago. I had a hole in my heart and I had no heart wall. I collapsed, but I was lucky that it happened in my doctor's surgery. My operation took place on a Wednesday and I was then unconscious until the Friday morning. The surgery lasted eight hours. I had to have it because it was the only chance I had of living.

I slightly remember being in ICU afterwards. I was on a ventilator and had a nurse beside my bed. I was also aware of my daughter coming in to hold my hand. I think it was on that first night that I had this experience.

I was in a state of peace and had a sense of floating. There was a beautiful azure-blue above me, along with stars. I felt a kind of healing, golden glow and was surrounded by love. It wasn't a white light, more like a golden-yellow sun. I never felt afraid or anxious or anything; instead, I felt very safe. I didn't leave my body. I was just in a beautiful place.

I felt I was surrounded by angels. That was the phrase I mentioned to one of the nurses afterwards. She was doing an evaluation of care and I described the experience I had by saying exactly that. They were the first impulsive words that came to my mind. But it wasn't that I actually saw the angels; it was just a feeling of being protected and that they were with me to see me through the surgery. I feel I was accompanied throughout.

As a child, I always prayed to my guardian angel. It was

more of a ritual then. When my children were being born, I would consciously pray for angels to be near me. I definitely believe they are beside you throughout life's voyage. I think intuition comes in part through your life's experience, but it also comes through guidance from that voice from elsewhere. And I think angels can intercede for you.

I have a very deep faith and I prayed before the operation. I asked for my body to be well and to survive the surgery. I had a lot of faith in the doctors, but I had faith in God as well, and I prayed that I would have more time with my family. I also feel that the love of our deceased relatives, or of other people we have lost, never ends. I believe we can talk to them and they will intercede. I believe that people who have loved you bring blessings to you.

What happened changed my life forever. It put my whole life in perspective. I feel I was very fortunate to have had the opportunity to have the surgery. Others haven't been so lucky to survive. I feel I was one of the lucky ones. I also had the privilege to have gone through the experience I had. In addition, I believe the prayers of my extended family got me through. I feel I am here by the grace of God.

EDEL, WHO COMES ORIGINALLY FROM COUNTY CARLOW **but who now lives in France, feels the presence of her deceased mother at all times. It's as if her mother is directing and guiding her life.**

My mother was a very typical Irish mother. She was intensely spiritual and our parish priest called her a 'hidden saint.' She was a very good person and she had been through a lot. Her only son had been killed back in 1986. I know her faith carried her through what happened. Although she had a bit of a nervous problem, she was very 'with it' at the same time.

In 2009, when she was 74, she went into hospital with a chest infection. I knew instinctively that she wasn't coming home and that she would die. As it happened, they found cancer in the lung. But she didn't die from the cancer; instead, she developed pneumonia and that's what killed her. They diagnosed her on a Wednesday and she died on the Friday. It was very quick.

She died on 9 October 2009. I think it was better that she was taken quickly rather than have a long-drawn-out illness. My father wouldn't have been able for it, nor would she. On her deathbed, she said she loved me but never understood me. I can understand why. I had a drink problem at the time. I also was going through a divorce and I was managing the farm. I had a rake of problems and my whole life was upside down.

My drinking got worse after she passed away. I was very upset and shaken. I was meant to go to various rehabs and I ended up in one of them the month after she died. I entered into rehab on 23 November. The programme was for three months, which seemed like an eternity to me, yet instinctively I knew that this was the place I was meant to be. Even before I went there, I knew it was right. When I passed through the door, I knew I was 'home'.

All the time in rehab, I knew my mother was with me. I knew she was there. It's hard to describe. I felt her presence. I also knew that this was the place she wanted me to go to. I knew she was carrying me through. I did my three months, knowing she was helping me all the time. From then on, I never looked back. I stopped smoking and stopped drinking. I now run mini-marathons. People ask me what my secret is, but it is hard to explain. Yet I know it has everything to do with my mother.

I came out of rehab and wondered, 'What do I do now?' I had graduated from college, but jobs were hard to get. The recession had started and there was no work. I was really at a big crossroads in my life. Once again, something strange happened and it determined my future. It ended in my coming to work in Lourdes.

What happened was that my mother had always been a big devotee of The Little Way Association, which has St. Thérèse of Lisieux as its patroness. Even though we had written to them and told them she had died, the magazines were still coming at home. One day, I was in the kitchen and I was reading one of the magazines. There was an ad for a job running a shop in Lourdes. I applied for it and I got it. That was in 2010.

When I arrived in Lourdes, again I instinctively knew this was where I was meant to be. Once more, I knew my mother had directed me and I felt her presence. I really felt she had brought me there, partly because of the way I had found the work and partly because it all felt so right. I automatically felt better.

I wasn't surprised by any of this because since she died my mother has been communicating with me in so many ways, both spiritually and physically. She has mostly been doing it indirectly. She does it in strange ways. Sometimes, I can smell her and I know she is in the room. I might be just in the kitchen and I can smell her. It's not a sweet aroma, but it is very distinctive, almost like soap. It's hard to describe.

There are also so many coincidences, which I know she brings about. For example, while in Lourdes, I always wanted to go on a pilgrimage, but I could never find a place on a tour. Then, one day, the strangest thing happened at work. I went off for lunch and locked the shop. The next thing, my neighbour rang me. She said, 'You are not going to believe this, but there are two people locked in your shop.' I thought it was a joke, but she said, 'I'm not joking. There are actually two people locked in the shop.' I couldn't believe it.

I returned back to the shop. It transpired that a nun had pushed in the door, closed it and it locked behind her and her friend. She was an Irish nun and was going to Lisieux on pilgrimage. It transpired that there was one place left on the pilgrimage and it was on the one date that suited me. So off I went to Lisieux. It was most amazing. I think my mother actually had the nun locked in the shop for me so that I couldn't miss her!

She has likewise been communicating with me through a medium I met here in France. She was a neighbour I just met up with. We got on great. I didn't even know she was a medium. She never told me that she had this gift. But, as time went on, she dropped hints. She started telling me how my mother was with me.

Through her, my mother advises me about family concerns. For example, my mother informed me that my dad would have a heart problem and shortly afterwards I got news that he had a heart blockage. I know that nobody else on this planet could have known the information that has been passed to me.

I could rattle off numerous examples of how my mother protects and guides me. By bringing me to France and giving me a total change of scene, she has allowed me to develop. I know she brought me here for a reason. It's not the route I would have chosen myself, but I am here. If she thinks that something is going to be good for me, or somebody is going to be good for me, she puts the opportunity in my way.

I am a different person from the person I was at the time she died. Every day, I get stronger and stronger. I think none of this is due to chance. It's just that she has never left me. I know she is here. I have no doubt about that at all. I see her in the way my life has unfolded. She drives me and drives my life. I feel privileged and honoured by what happens and to experience what I am experiencing. I believe she is with me all the time and will never leave me for the rest of my days.

THE VISIONS DEBATE

In 1949, two Harvard University researchers conducted a fascinating study of human perception. The purpose of the experiment was simple and clear. Are we, as human beings, receptive to new information even if it conflicts with everything we have previously believed in? Perhaps, to the contrary, we will do almost anything to overlook the new information in our attempts to uphold the established view. It was an intriguing investigation, not easy to construct, but the researchers – Jerome Bruner and Leo Postman – were up to the challenge.

The centrepiece of their study was a collection of ordinary playing cards like those you would expect to see in any standard deck. The researchers, however, pulled a fast one. Most of the cards were normal and printed in their proper colours, such as the ace of hearts or the seven of spades. Other cards, however, were rigged and they couldn't exist, including a black ace of diamonds and a red six of spades. All these cards were then shown briefly through a specially-designed visual display machine to a selection of 28 student volunteers.

The results were quite remarkable. The vast majority of volunteers identified all the cards as normal. They would refer to a red spade as either a heart or a spade, completely disregarding the fact that the card combined features of two incompatible suits. The unfamiliar was being repeatedly rejected. It simply could not exist. The volunteers were, in other words, misperceiving reality – rejecting crystal-clear evidence – because they could not accept that things so at odds with the norm might be real.

The investigators' main conclusion was unambiguous: 'For as long as possible and by whatever means available, the organism will ward off the perception of the unexpected, those things which do not fit his prevailing set.' Their initial assumption was proved: 'Most people come to depend upon a certain constancy in their environment and, save under special conditions, attempt to ward off variations from this state of affairs: "Thar ain't no such animal," the hayseed is reputed to have said on seeing his first giraffe.'

The world of science ought to cast an occasional eye on the research mentioned above, especially when it comes to deathbed visions. Although observed throughout the ages, chronicled across cultures, common to all religions and the subject of convincing research, these deathbed phenomena are at best completely ignored; at worst, scathingly dismissed by the mainstream scientific community.

Professor Carl B. Becker, Kyoto University, expresses the problem most succinctly: 'Scientists who are educated to be concerned with consistency find the survival data to be incompatible with their worldviews. By vigorously denying the existence and even the possibility of such data, they eliminate the data from their worldviews rather than modify their worldviews to fit the data.'

Deathbed visions cannot be real, science tells us, because they fly in the face of the long-established, widely-accepted laws and principles of scientific theory and research. As a result, multiple dismissive arguments are put forward to explain why visions of deceased family and friends, or visits from religious figures, can only 'appear' to happen. One of the most commonly articulated is that the visions are merely a form of wish-fulfilment – or wishful thinking – in which the dying conjure up images that they either expect or hope to witness as they pass away.

At first sight, the idea that the dying might act in this way seems compelling. Even if they have no firmly-entrenched religious belief system, they might revert to some ingrained or even primeval hope or wish that they are about to depart to an otherworld where they can be reconciled with people or religious figures of importance to them from their past. Although instantly appealing as a hypothesis, it is not borne out by the facts.

For a start, the most remarkable feature of the deathbed phenomenon is the extent of surprise and amazement shown by people who witness visions shortly before death. They frequently seem astonished – we might even say shocked – by what they are seeing. Those who observe them regularly remark on their sense of 'wonderment', as though they have been startled by something unforeseen or unanticipated. This palpable reaction – which has been identified throughout the ages and in multiple cultures – is far from the unsurprised response one would expect from people who had merely seen what they expected to see in the process of fulfilling or implementing wishes.

The concept of wish-fulfilment is likewise inadequate at describing the frequent surprise revealed at the physical appearance of the visiting figure. Expect to see particular physical characteristics and the likelihood is that you will. However, stories to the contrary are common. Among them is the vision experienced by the grandmother of American evangelist Billy Graham. On her deathbed, she sat up and said that she could see her dead husband Ben, who had been killed in a battle during the Civil War, in which he lost an eye and a leg. 'There is Ben,' the mystified woman exclaimed, 'and he has both of his eyes and both of his legs.'

A similar story is recalled by Sir William Barrett in *Death-Bed Visions*. This one concerns a dying man, John George, whose son had earlier been killed while working on the railroad. The dying man had been lying quietly in bed when he suddenly looked up. He opened wide his eyes and looked to the side of the bed where his wife, Mary Ann, was sitting. Speaking to her, the surprised man said: 'Here is Tom, and he is all right, no marks on him. Oh, he looks fine.' Shortly after that, Mr. George – whose expectations had clearly not been matched by what he had seen – died.

Even in cases involving angels or saints, surprise has also frequently been shown at the look, demeanour or dress of the arriving figures. As mentioned earlier on in this book, young children have commonly described angels as being without wings, contrary to long-established beliefs. In a further classic case, a young woman in her 20s who came close to death following complications in childbirth was taken aback by the appearance of her favourite saint, Gerard. Expecting to see him in fine velvet, he was dressed in the humble attire of a monk, with sandals and a grey gown. Once again, such are *not* the reactions of the dying achieving wish-fulfilment.

Let's return once more to the scientists who, as mentioned earlier, have launched many attempts to discredit deathbed visions from a medico-scientific perspective. Central to the majority of their arguments is the assertion that visions are mere hallucinations whereby those who are dying see people who simply aren't there. The images, they argue, are just inventions of the mind that are unreal and are therefore without significance in the context of what happens following death.

Before scrutinising their arguments in detail, a few general observations must be made. Unlike deathbed visions, which focus almost exclusively on visits from deceased family or friends or religious figureheads, hallucinations tend to contain a very wide range of elements including noises, voices, smells and tastes right through to a diverse range of disturbing visual images. Studies also show that whereas visions mostly relate to deceased people, very few deceased people appear during hallucinations.

There are further differences, too. Deathbed visions tend to be of a short duration, unlike hallucinations which may continue for hours. Visions also occur with the eyes open, while hallucinations can happen with them either open or closed. Most importantly, there is no clear-cut purpose to hallucinations, whereas deathbed visions have a specific intent – namely, the arrival of deceased family or friends or, to a lesser extent, religious figureheads to welcome the dying and to accompany them to the other side.

The scientific case, however, goes much deeper and requires additional scrutiny. Right at its core is the central tenet that the hallucinations experienced by the dying are just fantasies triggered by their troubled brains. The hallucinations, it is argued, can be prompted in any number of ways – by oxygen deprivation, sleep deprivation, drugs, fever, religious fervour and stress, for example. I will examine these and other factors in the following paragraphs.

The first proposition I will look at is that deathbed visions are mere hallucinations caused by a restricted flow of oxygen to the brain. The argument is very straightforward. The brain needs oxygen to survive and to function properly. Therefore, if the supply of oxygen is curtailed around the time of death, a person is likely to behave in a strange and abnormal way. They may hallucinate as well. Oxygen deprivation, sceptics argue, might in this way explain deathbed visions.

This proposition is badly flawed. Oxygen deprivation, when it occurs, mostly causes agitation and confusion. Other likely features include disorientation and mental turmoil. These are very much at odds with the calm, peace and serenity that normally accompany a deathbed vision. The two emotional states – distinct confusion in the case of oxygen deprivation; tranquillity in the case of deathbed visions – could hardly be more different.

In addition, general patients in a hospital or other setting who are clearly deprived of oxygen – perhaps suffering from severe asthma or heart failure – exhibit no particular tendency to report the arrival of deceased family or friends. You would expect them to do so if there was a direct causative connection between a shortage of oxygen to the brain and the most fundamental features of the deathbed vision. The case for a link between oxygen deprivation and deathbed visions must therefore be regarded as unsound.

Another theory proposes that deathbed visions are caused by hallucinations resulting from the interruptions to sleep patterns which may occur around the time of death. Sleep deprivation may lead to adverse effects on the brain. It is estimated that, depending on the amount of sleep that is lost, some 80 per cent of normal people will hallucinate. Perhaps, therefore, sleep-deprived people who are dying are merely imagining things that are not there.

There are complications, once more, with this proposition. The difficulties arise when we examine the nature of the hallucinations that take place. One typical study of sleep deprivation reported that, following three days, volunteers experienced things like spots before their eyes, moving wall tiles, jets of water on the floor – and, in one case, a strange, unknown frizzy-haired lady appearing in a hallway! Another study reported the appearance of dots, geometric patterns, wallpaper patterns and dreamlike distortions. These are entirely dissimilar to the general features of deathbed visions, thus ruling out a connection.

Many other potential causative factors might arise in the days or hours before death, including the administration of drugs, the presence of a high fever or problems associated with levels of consciousness. They could also cause the dying to hallucinate and must be assessed. These issues are nowhere better tackled than in the landmark investigation of deathbed visions published in 1977 by researchers Dr. Karlis Osis and Dr. Erlendur Haraldsson.

Their study, *At the Hour of Death*, which spanned many years of research and three comprehensive surveys, involved 50,000 terminally-ill patients who were observed shortly before their deaths by 1,000 doctors and nurses. It was the first – and it remains the most important – genuinely scientific inquiry into the experiences of the dying. Their investigations were all the more crucial in that they covered two very different countries, the USA and India, or West and East. Their conclusions will be scrutinised and referred to extensively in the following paragraphs.

To begin with, it can be reasonably argued that certain sedative or intoxicating drugs may have hallucinatory effects and, as a result, cause visions. This is a popular argument. However, the 'drugs-explain-all' thesis can be immediately dismissed. What if the dying who experience deathbed visions are either on no drugs whatsoever or on drugs prescribed in inconsequential amounts? This question was addressed by Osis and Haraldsson.

Of those who had experienced deathbed visions in their study and whose medication history was known, some 61 per cent had received no sedation at all. A further 19 per cent had received drugs in such small doses, or drugs so mild, that they were regarded by those who administered them as being inconsequential. In other words, a total of 80 per cent of dying patients who had apparition experiences could not have been influenced by drugs. 'It seems safe to conclude that most of our patients' visionary experiences were not caused by drug intoxication,' the researchers concluded.

Hallucinations might also result from a high fever, with elevated temperatures causing delirium. As a result, people might invent strange people or hear voices. They might also imagine fantastic scenarios or conjure up bizarre scenes. Perhaps, then, situations where deceased relatives or friends are perceived to arrive at the time of death may be the product of febrile brains.

This issue was likewise scrutinised by Osis and Haraldsson. Some 58 per cent of those for whom details were available had temperatures within the normal range. An additional 34 per cent had only low-grade fevers. Taken together, these two percentages represent more than nine out of ten people who experienced visions. Only eight per cent of patients had what were rated as high temperatures. The authors concluded: 'In only a very minor portion of the patients does it seem possible that the apparitions could have been caused by fever.'

Osis and Haraldsson went on to investigate an additional potential cause of visions, namely the consciousness or awareness levels of those passing away. The dying can experience any number of different states of consciousness ranging from being comatose, with very low consciousness levels, to being highly alert. They may dream peacefully or become delirious. Awareness levels may also fluctuate wildly. On the surface, at least, consciousness may have a role to play.

In this case, the researchers found that at the time the patients in their study had their deathbed visions, approximately one-half were in a clear state of consciousness and fully aware of their surrounding environments. A further one-third were mildly impaired, but could still be communicated with. Less than one-fifth were severely impaired. They concluded: 'According to the judgement of the physicians and nurses we interviewed, the majority of the patients who had these visionary experiences were in a normal, wakeful state of consciousness.'

One of the most hotly-debated assertions made regarding deathbed visions is that they merely reflect the religious convictions of those who experience them. Belief that an afterlife exists where we will meet familiar deceased figures is for all practical purposes universal and a feature of virtually all religions. Right back to our early Neanderthal forebears, the presumption existed that upon death we travelled from the land of the living to a land of the dead. There, we would all meet again.

The Book of Genesis, which is the first book of the Hebrew Bible (Tanakh) and the Christian Old Testament, incorporates many references to afterlife reconciliations. Abraham, after he died at a 'good old age,' was said to have been 'gathered to his people' – in other words, been reconciled with those of his race who had passed on before him. The same was said to have happened with Jacob, Isaac and Ishmael. King David, in the Book of Samuel, after he lost his child, was overcome by sadness, but was comforted by the belief that they would meet again. 'I shall go to him,' he said.

The legendary Greek philosopher Socrates, who lived from 469 – 399 BC, spoke of a place we travel to after death which is 'inhabited by the spirits of departed men.' The Roman philosopher Cicero, who lived from 106 – 43 BC, wrote that he hoped to meet beloved friends among a similar 'divine congregation of departed spirits.' Preconditioning like this, so intense and stretching back so far, some sceptics argue, paves the way for and explains both deathbed visions and near-death experiences.

Contrary to this argument, however, what happens with deathbed visions – along with near-death experiences, to which they are so closely related – diverges extensively from what might be anticipated. For a start, both atheists and agnostics – not just the religiously-attuned – are among those who report the arrival of deceased figures around the time of death. This, perhaps, is the greatest surprise as they have no expectation of supernatural visits. The oddness that someone should be coming to meet them when they are dying doesn't appear to cross their minds.

In addition, a surprising number of people – especially in the case of near-death experiences – are loath to describe the religious figures they witness in the conventional manner construed by established religions. For example, they seldom refer to them in terms of 'beards', 'long hair', 'white robes' or the manner in which Jesus, Mary, Shiva, Vishnu or other figures are usually depicted in religious art. Instead, they normally describe a 'superior being' with 'great compassion', 'enormous intelligence', 'wisdom' and 'kindness' who they 'know' or 'sense' to be God. This, again, flies in the face of the indoctrination proposition.

This issue of religion was also examined in the Osis and Haraldsson study and the insights they gleaned are worth mentioning. All main religious affiliations were represented on the USA side of the investigation, including the Protestant, Catholic, Jewish and other much-less-supported faiths. Also included were people with little or no faith at all. Hindus, Christians and Muslims were represented on the Indian side of the study.

Their conclusions were most interesting. The percentages of people representing different faiths having visions in both countries pretty closely matched the percentages representing the different faiths in the populations in general. It was clear, therefore, that a person's particular faith had little or no bearing on whether a deathbed vision would be experienced. 'It appears that the kind of religious affiliation was not a determining factor in the occurrence of this phenomenon,' the authors concluded.

There were two additional factors – stress and expectations of death – that were examined in the Osis and Haraldsson study and both are worth noting. Stress, which can cause moodiness, agitation, lack of concentration and physical deterioration, can clearly be present in the days or hours prior to death. The pain associated with many medical conditions and illnesses can act as a major stressor, as can the general process of dying and the environment in which the act takes place.

Seeking an indicator of stress, the researchers documented patients' moods in the day preceding their visions. Their assumption was very simple – a 'bad' mood, involving anger, anxiety or depression, would identify the likely existence of stress; a 'normal' or 'average' mood would, by comparison, indicate the relative absence of stress. The results again were clear. Stress had no role to play. In fact, it would appear that those with normal moods – in other words, those less under stress – had the greatest capacity to experience visions.

On the issue of people's expectations about death, the study's conclusions were similarly clear and unambiguous. The authors postulated that those expecting to die might be prone to indulge in otherworld fantasies to assuage their fears of what was to come. By way of contrast, those who were expected to live might be much less inclined to do so. It turned out that expectations of death had no role to play. They concluded: 'It seems that apparitions show a purpose of their own, contradicting the intentions of the patients. This suggests that they are not merely outward projections from the patient's psyche.'

Strangely, on this issue, the authors encountered several cases where, despite a patient's good prognosis, the occurrence of the vision signalled a hasty demise. One case they chronicled involved a man whose doctor's predictions were positive and whose own confident expectation and wish was that he would survive. Suddenly, he exclaimed, 'Somebody is calling me.' Soon afterwards, he assured relatives, 'Don't worry. I will be all right.' Ten minutes later, he died. Clearly, whoever it was that called from afar was more closely tuned in to the patient's prognosis than either the doctor or the patient himself!

The question remains then: what causes deathbed visions? No answer exists. All we can accurately say is that profound medico-scientific explanations will not be discovered by looking at religious fervour or wish-fulfilment, or revealed by scrutinising diverse issues such as oxygen deprivation, sleep deprivation, drugs, fever or fluctuating levels of consciousness. Nor will explanations be discovered by focusing on factors such as stress or expectations of death. Just as science cannot accommodate the possibility that deathbed visions might be real, nor can it explain them away.

A comparable dilemma exists for the scientific community when it comes to assessing near-death experiences or, more specifically, in the case of the theme of this book, that aspect of them involving meetings with deceased relatives and friends or well-established religious figureheads. Just as with deathbed visions, many explanations are put forward. Some have a familiar ring – notably oxygen deprivation, drugs, wishful thinking and religious fervour. Since these have been touched on already, there is no need to go into them again.

It is worth mentioning, however, regarding the potential implication of drugs, that a large proportion of near-death experiences – resulting from, for example, sudden heart attacks, car crashes or perhaps a near-drowning – take place in non-medical settings where no medication whatsoever is involved, rendering the drug argument redundant. Likewise, the agitation, mental turmoil, disorientation and memory loss that occur in the case of oxygen deprivation are far removed from the peace, tranquillity and vivid memory retention generally associated with near-death experiences.

Further theories have been proposed, with many taking an entirely different tack from the explanations postulated for deathbed visions. Although these have been examined extensively in *Going Home* and *The Distant Shore*, some are worth revisiting. In essence, all conclude that the near-death phenomenon has nothing to do with an afterlife and a lot to do with hallucinations induced by our malfunctioning bodies and brains as we shut down prior to death.

One analysis, published by Slovenian scientists in 2010, proposed that the phenomenon may be caused by raised levels of carbon dioxide in the blood. Their conclusion followed from a research evaluation they conducted of cardiac arrest patients who had near-death experiences. Unfortunately for this theory, however, high carbon dioxide levels are also associated with good resuscitations, and patients with good resuscitations tend to better recall their experiences. It is more likely, therefore, that survivors with high blood carbon dioxide levels merely have sharper memories of their near-death experiences.

Another scientific investigation, this time emanating from George Washington University, Washington DC, postulated that surges of electrical activity observed in patients shortly before they passed away may cause the evocative mental sensations associated with near-death experiences. Again, although the electrical surges undoubtedly had occurred, no connection whatsoever was established between them and the near-death phenomenon if only because all those in the study died, with the result that we cannot know what they experienced. The study, involving just seven volunteers, was also small.

A further argument, from the scientist and astronomer Carl Sagan, asserted that what we experience at death is merely a mirror-image of what occurs at birth. In other words, the tunnel, bright light and the friendly faces of a near-death experience are just a replica of the birth canal, delivery-room lights and smiling faces of the parents and medical staff during childbirth. However, a study of people who had near-death experiences and who were born through Caesarean section – where no birth canal is involved – found that they reported tunnel travel in almost exactly the same proportion as those born naturally, thus killing the theory stone dead.

An additional proposition suggests that the natural pain-killing chemicals known as endorphins may be responsible for all the pleasant sensations reported during near-death experiences. These chemicals are released by the brain at times of stress, so why not at the time of death? There is, however, no proof that the brain generates a significantly greater quantity of endorphins as we expire. In fact, the evidence suggests that they are present in similar amounts at other stressful times in our lives. Why, then, don't we have near-death experiences on these occasions and not just at the time of death?

A final proposal worth mentioning, originating from the University of Kentucky, involves a condition some people suffer from surrounding sleep. During Rapid Eye Movement (REM) sleep, we dream the most, but we also are paralysed, with only our eye muscles, heart, some other muscles including those controlling our blood vessels and intestines, and our diaphragm which is vital in controlling our breathing, being spared from the paralysis.

Some people, however, suffer from REM intrusion, where a person's mind wakes up before their body paralysis ends, resulting in hallucinations and a feeling of detachment from the body. This, according to the study, could explain much of what we know about the near-death experience.

'I treat all of these experiences with the reverence and respect they deserve,' Professor Kevin Nelson, who conducted the aforementioned study, says of the near-death experience case histories he has encountered. 'I might be trying to explain how and why they happen in physiological terms, but I would argue that isn't incompatible with people believing in God if they want to. After all, who's to say that these mechanisms weren't created by God in the first place precisely to provide comfort just when we might need it most – as we approach death.'

Returning exclusively to deathbed visions, this still leaves the question of their role in establishing the case for survival following death. It has long been believed that of all death phenomena – including near-death experiences, out-of-body travel, apparitions or other visitations – deathbed visions provide the most convincing support for the existence of an afterlife. Not only are the visions profoundly real to those who are dying, but the events are commonly witnessed by others, transcend all cultures and eras and are experienced by people of both sexes and all ages and creeds. They are also consistent in content and have a common intent.

Most pertinently, cases where the dying report visits from deceased people who they could not have known had died have a compelling authenticity. Numerous examples have been recorded through the centuries, right up to the present day. They defy any rational explanation and raise serious questions about how those who are dying have ascertained their facts. Such cases have serious implications for the potential existence of life after death.

How can sceptics explain these extraordinary cases away? The answer is they explain them away badly. They frequently counter-argue that the dying person must have come into possession of the information telepathically. In other words, news about the otherwise-unknown death must have been transferred telepathically from the person who earlier died to the person now experiencing the deathbed vision.

Alternatively, they claim, the information must have taken an indirect route through another person, a third-party, who telepathically passed it on. It is ironic how sceptics who put forward these explanations, most of whom are unconvinced about life after death, should reach to another paranormal phenomenon – namely, extrasensory perception – to explain away deathbed visions where previously-unknown information is so inexplicably gleaned!

The inability to dismiss these remarkable cases, along with their intrinsic credibility, has led many esteemed individuals to reach forceful conclusions. As far back as the beginning of the twentieth century, Professor Charles Richet, who was a Nobel Prize winner in 1913 and a sceptic of afterlife claims, adjudged that they constituted strong evidence for survival. In his celebrated book *Thirty Years of Psychical Research*, he expressed it this way: 'Among all the facts adduced to prove survival, these seem to me to be the most disquieting.'

It is a view to which Sir William Barrett was also drawn, not only because of cases he encountered when compiling his iconic book *Death-Bed Visions*, but also from other examples chronicled in his work *On the Threshold of the Unseen* and from further stories he came across through the Society for Psychical Research. Writing in the 1920s, Barrett concluded: 'The evidence of visions of the dying, when they appear to see and recognise some of their relatives of whose decease they were unaware, affords perhaps one of the strongest arguments in favour of survival.'

The researchers Osis and Haraldsson reached corresponding conclusions from their broad-ranging study of the deathbed phenomenon. Following close scrutiny of dying visions, they argued that neither medical, nor psychological, nor cultural conditioning could explain deathbed visions away. Only the existence of life after death explained the data they collected, they argued. As they put it: 'We feel that the total body of information makes possible a fact-based, rational, and therefore realistic belief in life after death.'

But are these individuals right? For many who witness these scenes at bedsides, that question is already answered.

Although often stunned by what they are seeing, they are heartened that their loved ones have achieved peace in their final hours. Likewise, they are reassured that those who are departing are not alone and lonely. They are also glad to have been shown that the death process may not be as dark and fearsome as is commonly believed, but instead may be a tranquil journey in which deceased family and friends escort those who are dying to the other side.

For those who are doing the dying, the impact of the experience seems to be even more profound. Clearly, for them, the images they see are real. Focused ahead, they gaze and stare intently, with eyes fixed, attention firmly latched onto the deceased relatives or friends they are so pleased to meet. Happiness lights up their eyes. Calmness descends and all pain disappears. Agitation, disquiet and distress ebb away and are replaced by a calm serenity. They are enveloped by a warm sense of joy. The process of dying is no longer a struggle, more a journey home.

ACKNOWLEDGEMENTS

This book ultimately belongs to the contributors who described their loved ones' deathbed visions. They were most courageous to speak out. Unfortunately, the phenomenon, although commonly observed, remains hidden, concealed, burrowed away. Like most death-related topics, it is dismissed, disregarded and spoken of rarely. To those who were willing to surmount these barriers and to share their stories, I am sincerely grateful.

In the course of my research, I spoke with hundreds of people from all corners of Ireland, north and south. Among them were Roman Catholics, Methodists, Presbyterians and members of the Church of Ireland and Jewish faiths. Others came from recent immigrant groups, reflecting disparate religious persuasions. While most were moderately spiritual, some were strong believers; others had no faith whatsoever. All ages and both sexes were represented. To each and every one, I am thankful.

On the books front, although other studies have been compiled over the years, none ranks more highly than Sir William Fletcher Barrett's *Death-Bed Visions*, which was published in 1926. Barrett was a truly remarkable man: a Jamaica-born scientist who arrived in Ireland in 1873, having been appointed as Professor of Physics at the Royal College of Science in Dublin. The college, at the time, had yet to be absorbed into UCD, where it eventually formed the basis of the Science Faculty.

Barrett was a brilliant scientist and avowed Christian, who committed himself to helping Dublin's poor and its educationally deprived. Soon after his arrival, he developed an interest in spiritualism and issues pertaining to life after death. He also wrote some wonderful books, including *On the Threshold of the Unseen*, *Psychical Research* and his seminal *Death-Bed Visions*, which was published a year after his death. I am indebted to this extraordinary pioneer of the afterlife, whose books are essential reading to this day.

Another historic text worth noting is the impressive *The Peak in Darien* by Anglo-Irish author Frances Power Cobbe. Published in 1882, the book incorporates a fascinating essay detailing the author's reflections on the deathbed phenomenon. The text also contains some intriguing case histories. 'Were I permitted to record with names and references half the instances of this occurrence which have been narrated to me, this short essay might have been swelled to a volume,' the author remarks in this invaluable source.

Additional priceless books were written by Dr. James H. Hyslop, who was Professor of Logic and Ethics at Columbia University and a prominent psychical researcher in the early twentieth century. Among his works are *Psychical Research and the Resurrection*, published in 1908, *Psychical Research and Survival*, published in 1913, and *Contact with the Other World*, published in 1919. Initially a sceptic and founder of the American Institute for Scientific Research, he became one of the most respected psychical investigators of all time. His books are wonderful for their insights and real-life examples from the past.

Turning to more recent times, *At the Hour of Death* by Dr. Karlis Osis and Dr. Erlendur Haraldsson is without any doubt the most authoritative and truly comprehensive work available to scholars and general readers alike. Based on three surveys conducted in the USA and India, the book, which was initially published in 1977, marks the earliest scientific investigation of the dying experience. Employing modern research techniques, the authors use a mixture of factual data and illustrative case histories to powerful effect. As investigations go of what takes place during the hours preceding death, it may never be surpassed.

An additional highly-regarded resource is Professor Carl B. Becker's *Paranormal Experience and Survival of Death*, which examines an extensive collection of arguments and counter-arguments concerning the hereafter. Based on data and surveys stretching back over a century, and using material from four continents, Becker's work is clear, comprehensive, reputable and impartial. It is an excellent study of all aspects of paranormal phenomena, including deathbed visions.

Professor Ian Currie's *You Cannot Die* also draws from an extensive range of accumulated research and provides a very useful introduction to the main issues of death survival. His succinct chapter on the deathbed phenomenon, which covers everything from the nature of visitations to childhood case histories, religious apparitions and possible explanations, is accompanied by further chapters on out-of-body experiences, hauntings and reincarnation, among many other topics. This introductory work is worth reading.

As a chronicle of real-life stories from the USA, David Kessler's book *Visions, Trips, and Crowded Rooms: Who and What You See Before You Die* is an excellent addition to the literature and should also be read. As Kessler puts it, his book is 'a report from the front lines, featuring stories of average people, in their own words, experiencing extraordinary events.' There are contributions from many healthcare professionals, along with clergy and those who have lost loved ones. Adding to its authenticity are the many non-believers and sceptics who are featured within.

Although the book restricts itself to near-death experiences, *Glimpses of Heaven* by Mally Cox-Chapman is a further valuable read. Does heaven exist? What is it like? While these are some of the fundamental questions it tackles, the book also examines issues such as reunions in heaven, who will guide us there and the question of whether we will meet those we love. Based on interviews with more than 50 people, this is a well-thought-out exposition of many of the topics relating to the afterlife discussion.

Before departing from books, a brief list of other works of possible interest to readers includes *Parting Visions* by Melvin Morse and Paul Perry, *When the Dying Speak* by Ron Wooten-Green, *One Last Hug Before I Go* by Carla Wills-Brandon and *Crossing the Threshold of Eternity* by Robert L. Wise. Each of these, in one way or another, covers the main theme of this current book. All are in print, as paperbacks, and can be relatively easily purchased.

There were other invaluable sources used in the course of my research which need to be credited. In particular, I am grateful to Jerome Bruner and Leo Postman of Harvard University for their 1949 study *On the Perception of Incongruity: A Paradigm*, which was referred to in the opening of The Visions Debate chapter. Another good general article, providing a useful overview, was Dr. R. Craig Hogan's *Near-Death Awareness as Evidence for Survival*. This brief document can be accessed online.

My sincere gratitude also goes to the Society for Psychical Research, which was established in London in 1882. An esteemed society, it was the first to conduct organised scholarly research into the paranormal. Among its early members were Professor Henry Sidgwick of Cambridge

University, classical scholar Frederic Myers, philosopher and Prime Minister Arthur Balfour, psychologist Sigmund Freud, the poet William Butler Yeats and Sir William Barrett. Its journal and proceedings, and in particular its now-iconic study *Phantasms of the Living*, are priceless resources from an earlier age.

A number of individuals also need to be thanked for their assistance in the production and design of this book. Linda Monahan, from Typeform, designed the cover with her usual creative flair and skill. Typeform's Pat Conneely, who laid out the text, was a pleasure to work with, as was the company's efficient production director Roy Thewlis. Weeshie Fogarty, who is a great friend and enthusiast, along with Monica O'Shea and Helen Keane, were of more assistance than they could ever imagine. My appreciation also goes to Kathleen O'Connor, who was generous as always with her observations and sound advice.

I am also indebted to Professor Donal Hollywood and his team at St. Luke's Hospital in Dublin, not to mention his ever-helpful assistant Bernadette O'Sullivan. Without them, this book would never have been written. Likewise, I wish to express my gratitude to Professor Con Timon, Dr. John Kennedy, Dr. Nemer Osman, Linda Weekes and Therese Harvey, all of St. James's Hospital in Dublin.

Finally, I would like to acknowledge Úna O'Hagan for her priceless support. From the book's initial conception to its arrival in bookshops, she was a tireless source of inspiration and energy. She also helped with the onerous task of proof-reading the text. I cannot overemphasise her contribution in bringing this undertaking to fruition and hopefully in re-establishing the deathbed vision as an issue for discussion and debate.

GOING HOME

IRISH STORIES FROM THE EDGE OF DEATH

Colm Keane

Going Home contains the most comprehensive insights ever provided by Irish people into what happens when we die.

Many of those interviewed have clinically died – some after heart attacks, others after long illnesses or accidents. They have returned to claim – 'There is life after death!'

Most have travelled through dark tunnels and entered intensely bright lights. Some have been greeted by dead relatives and met a superior being. All have floated outside their bodies and watched themselves down below.

Those left behind describe visions of relatives who passed away. The book also acquaints us with the latest scientific research.

Award-winning journalist Colm Keane has spoken to people from all corners of Ireland and recounts their stories.

Based on years of research, Going Home provides us with the most riveting insight we may ever get into where we go after death.

Reviews of *Going Home*

'Fascinating' *Irish Daily Mail*

'Intriguing' *Sunday World*

'A beautiful, satisfying, comforting book' *Radio Kerry*

THE DISTANT SHORE

MORE IRISH STORIES FROM THE EDGE OF DEATH

Colm Keane

The Distant Shore is packed with a wealth of new Irish stories about life after death.

Extraordinary accounts of what takes place when we die are featured throughout. Reunions with deceased relatives and friends, and encounters with a 'superior being', are included.

Visions of dead family members are described. The book also examines astonishing premonitions of future events.

This compilation was inspired by the huge response to Colm Keane's number one bestseller Going Home – a groundbreaking book that remained a top seller for six months.

Containing new material and insights, The Distant Shore is indispensable reading for those who want to know what happens when we pass away.

Reviews of *The Distant Shore*

'Amazing new stories' *Irish Independent*
'Terrific, wonderful read' *Cork 103 FM*
'A source of genuine comfort to anyone who has suffered a bereavement' *Western People*